Walks with Rich

A Personal Tribute to Rich Mullins

C.W. Hambleton

Walks with Rich
Copyright © 2015 by C.W. Hambleton

Connect with Me Online:
Website: http://www.cwhambleton.com
Facebook: http://facebook.com/cwhambleton
Goodreads: http://goodreads.com/cwhambleton
Twitter: http://twitter.com/chris_hambleton
Blog: http://fictionsoftware.wordpress.com

Discover Other Titles by the Author

Speculative Fiction Titles
"Out of the Whirlwind"
"The Exchange"
"The Castors of Giza"
"The Cell"
"Endeavor in Time"

The Time of Jacob's Trouble Trilogy
"The Last Aliyah" (Book 1)
"The Son of Shinar" (Book 2)
"The Siege of Zion" (Book 3)

The Sons of Liberty Trilogy
"The Convention" (Book 1)
"The Green Zone" (Book 2)
"The Declaration" (Book 3)

The Days of Noah Series
"Rise of the Anshar" (Book 1)

The HaZikaron Series
"The Seed of Haman" (Book 1)

Non-Fiction Titles
"Walks with Rich"
"Our American Awakening"
"The American Tyrant"
"Ezekiel Watch"
"On the Precipice"

The playlist for all songs in this book are at:
http://tinyurl.com/WalksWithRichSongs

To discover more about Rich Mullins and his music, please visit KidBrothers.net.

To learn more about C.W. Hambleton and his other books, please visit his author website at http://www.cwhambleton.com.

Table of Contents

"Sometimes I am tempted to believe that I am better than anybody because I know Him. And then I remember that I don't know him because I was smart enough to figure out some riddle. And I don't know him because I was good enough to ascend into heaven on my own and shake hands with him and meet him. Of all the things that make God awesome, the most awesome thing in the world that I can imagine from a god is that one who would be holy, and one that would be just, and one that would be innocent and beautiful, and would have no need of me – that someone like that could love me is amazing. And that does not make me a good person, but it makes Him a great God!" – Rich Mullins, June 25, 1994

Foreword

"I think it's very hard to allow God to break us. I think it's very hard to be broken. And I think that who the Lord loves He chastens, and that if we'll never be broken we'll never be saved. And that God doesn't break us because He hates us, or because He's angry at us, but we have to be broken, just like you have to break a horse." – Rich Mullins, September 15, 1990

Rich Mullins was one of the formative voices in early contemporary Christian music, and though he left the stage more than fifteen years ago, his songs still speak to countless people across the world.

I honestly don't remember where I first heard Rich's music, but it was probably on KLOV or another Christian radio station. Most likely, the song was "Awesome God" or "Brother's Keeper," but since that was about twenty years ago, I'm entitled to a slightly spotty memory. Sometimes "Awesome God" and "Step by Step" are still sung in contemporary churches as part of their worship repertoire, but his songs are seldom played on the airwaves now.

It wasn't merely Rich's melodies that first captured my interest years ago, but the spiritual depth and painful honesty in his songs. After I bought an album or two and learned more about him, I was surprised to find that we came from similar backgrounds, with both of us growing up on farms in Amish/Mennonite country in the Indiana/Ohio area. I was surprised that we also shared the same middle name, "Wayne" which I've always rather disliked, though he embraced it. I suppose it was the simple, quiet farm-life and the salt-of-the-earth people who molded Rich into the man he became, and glimpses of those origins are very evident in many of his songs, particularly "First Family" and "Boy Like Me/Man Like You."

After I discovered the music of Rich Mullins, I ended up purchasing all his albums except for his first one "Behold the Man" with his college-band "Zion." Some of those early songs were recorded on other albums though, such as "Praise to the Lord," "Hope to Carry On," and "Heaven in His Eyes." His posthumous albums "The Jesus Record" and "The Jesus Demos" have been a particular blessing to me, though I tend to prefer the rough demo recordings to the professionally-produced songs. It's a bit eerie at times to realize that those demos were among the last songs he ever sung.

Oddly enough, it wasn't Rich's more popular songs that drew me to his music as much as the B-Sides, the songs that were rarely (if ever) played on the radio. It is in those songs that much of his life, soul, and relationship with God are revealed. Rich always did seem like a B-sides kind of guy, not wanting to draw much attention to himself or conform to whatever was popular as much as sharing his music with others wherever and however he could. Every Christian has their own personal ministry or calling in this world, and this was his.

I first began listening to his songs soon after meeting my ex-wife in 1996, and Rich died a couple of months after we were married in 1997. Though I had never met him, I felt like I had almost lost a brother. He passed away just as the Internet was taking off (though before YouTube and digital cameras), so few of his concerts/clips are available. The recent movie "Ragamuffin" revealed many of his personal struggles with alcoholism and loneliness that were often echoed in his songs. If you listen closely enough, you can almost hear the brokenness in his music.

Rich never married (though he wanted to), yet he accepted his life of singleness and celibacy, which were also expressed as brokenness and yearnings in his songs. As my marriage has broken up over the past year, his songs have meant more to me than ever before. Though many of them have always had special meaning to me, it wasn't until I was broken that they became especially dear to my heart. There are times when I'm listening to his songs at work or in the car and I find myself overwhelmed with emotions. Many Christians often shy away from being honest about their personal struggles, but not Rich – his struggles came out in his music.

Over the last year, I have been spiritually and emotionally broken as never before, yet God has never felt so real to me as He is now. The most important lessons in life cannot be taught but must be experienced, those lessons that can only be learned through brokenness and suffering and sorrow. It's not in the good times that overcomers are made, but in the dark times, the days when everything is crashing and burning all around you and threatening to drag you down into the pit of despair. Character is forged in the fires of affliction and adversity, not in comfort and pleasure. Patience and perseverance are learned when there's no other option. Humility and dependence upon God are learned in the cold, lonely bed of brokenness.

Coincidentally, Rich died a month before his 42nd birthday, and the final stake was driven into my marriage shortly before my 42nd birthday as well. As I go forward, a new life of uncertainty, brokenness, and likely loneliness awaits, which I find particularly frightening at times when I look further ahead than I should. Loneliness was something Rich frequently struggled with, and to that I can relate.

This book isn't a devotional as much as a personal tribute to the man and his music that has influenced me more deeply

than any other musician has. This literary tribute to Rich
Mullins is about putting into words the tremendous impact
his music has had on my faith and what it has personally
meant to me over the years, as well as the healing and hope
his songs have helped bring by pointing to God in the midst
of this broken world. This is without a doubt my most
personal book, and I'm afraid that it may not mean all that
much to you unless you've been broken in spirit and have
come to depend on God just to get through the day
sometimes (or many times!).

One of my favorite pastimes is to take long walks
(typically at least a half-hour or so), and I've enjoyed taking
walks probably as far back as fifth or sixth grade in
elementary school. My childhood home in Ohio was
surrounded by woods and fields, and whenever I was bored
or needed a change of scenery, I walked. Taking walks
meant being able to take a break and think, dream, and pray
and just drink in what was around me. Today, I often listen
to Rich's music when I walk our two dogs, and those are the
times his music has touched me the most.

The songs in this book are my personal favorites, many of
which have grown on me over the years and many miles. Of
the twenty-five songs listed, I would have to say that my
"Best of the Best" are "Be With You," "The Breaks," and
"The Love of God." I've had the song "Both Feet on the
Ground" continually playing through my head for months
because it's beautiful and romantic and it always reminds
me that though I'm alone now, I'll be alright because God is
by my side.

The format of this book is song-centric; each of these
B-side favorites has its own chapter with the lyrics and its
personal meaning to me and related insights. You won't find
many of Rich's more popular songs here like "Awesome
God" or "Praise to the Lord," but you will find many of his
greatest ones, the ones that bear his heart and soul. As
depicted in the "Ragamuffin" movie, Rich seemed to enjoy

playing the B-sides more than his most popular songs like "Awesome God" anyway, preferring to just get the popular ones out of the way so he could settle in and really connect with his audience.

Also, this book is written from a predominantly Christian perspective and assumes the reader has a basic knowledge of the Bible and mainstream Christian theology. Given the Christian nature of Rich's songs, it would be difficult (if not impossible) to understand or interpret them with any other perspective. Though Rich struggled with many things in this life, he always clung to his faith in our Lord Jesus Christ, the Author and Finisher of our faith. Perhaps the best way to really read this book is to listen to each song before reading the chapter. The YouTube playlist can be found at: http://tinyurl.com/WalksWithRichSongs

I had never planned to write this book, but it quickly became one that simply had to be written. Rich's music has been such a big part of my life for such a long time, and I can't think of any greater influence on how I see God and the world around me (with the exception of the Bible, of course). I doubt that any other time in my life could produce the brokenness needed to adequately express what Rich's songs really mean to me. Like olives or grapes in a press, it's in the crushing that one's spirit is revealed.

If these clumsy words can minister to others in their times of sorrow and brokenness or just speak to them in some meaningful way, then that's the greatest blessing I could ever ask for.

In His Grace,
Chris Hambleton

Walks With Rich

1. All the Way My Savior Leads Me

"People always say, 'I don't know where the Lord is leading me.' I always say, 'It don't really make a whole lot of difference.' The important thing is to be where He has led you to already. If He has led you into a marriage, then be faithful there. If He has led you into being single, then be faithful there. If He has blessed you with many material goods, then be a good steward of those goods. And if He has blessed you by allowing you to imitate His life of poverty, then imitate it with great joy." – Rich Mullins

"All the Way My Savior Leads Me" is a little-known acoustic song from one of Rich's early albums that was adapted from the hymn by Fanny Crosby. The hymn is still played in traditional churches, and though the words may be the same, the melody is much different between Rich's version and the hymn. Personally, I much prefer Rich's adaptation, which throws me off whenever we sing the hymn in church.

Whenever I hear Rich's version of this song, I always picture a quiet, winding path through an old country woods like the ones I explored growing up. The words of Psalm 23 are whispering in the wind, and a gentle breeze is rustling the changing leaves and the tall grass nearby.

As one of Rich's slower songs, often when I hear it I cannot help but be reminded to slow down from my frequently hectic schedule, stop running around for a moment, and simply wait upon the Lord and His leading.

Some of the busiest people I know are those involved in the church, and how often He gets lost in the midst of our well-intentioned busyness! Remember what Jesus accused the Church of Ephesus of in Revelation 2:1-7, that *"they had forgotten their first love."* They were doing everything right except that which really mattered the most: loving Christ and loving one another. How often and easy it is to be so busy about our Master's business that we forget about the Master Himself?

Proverbs 16:9 declares that *"A man's heart plans his way, but the Lord directs his steps."* For we who are called by His name, one of the hardest things to do in our modern lives of busyness is to realize that we are the spiritual equivalent of sheep who are often anxious, aimless, and need to be led by the Good Shepherd for our own good. The Lord has one simple command that He proclaims throughout the Bible: *"Follow me!"*

All the Way My Savior Leads Me
Rev 7:17

All the way my Savior leads me
What have I to ask beside?
Can I doubt His faithful mercies?
Who through life has been my guide
Heavenly peace, divinest comfort
Ere by faith in Him to dwell
For I know whate'er fall me
Jesus doeth all things well

All of the way my Savior leads me
And He cheers each winding path I tread
Gives me strength for every trial
And He feeds me with the living bread
And though my weary steps may falter

And my soul a-thirst may be
Gushing from a rock before me
Though a spirit joy I see

And all the way my Savior leads me
Oh, the fullness of His love
Perfect rest in me is promised
In my Father's house above
When my spirit clothed immortal
Wings its flight through the realms of the day
This my song through endless ages
Jesus led me all the way

"All The Way My Savior Leads Me" was originally written by Fanny Crosby, one of the most prolific songwriters in history. Though blind from early childhood, Crosby wrote over 8,000 Christian hymns. When asked of her handicap, she said, "If perfect earthly sight were offered me tomorrow I would not accept it. I might not have sung hymns to the praise of God if I had been distracted by the beautiful and interesting things about me."

Of all the physical handicaps, I personally feel that blindness would be the most difficult because of its debilitating nature and the inherent dependency on others. Even being blindfolded for a few moments can be a frightening experience, especially in unfamiliar surroundings. Spiritually speaking, though we may have excellent sight and think we see quite clearly, all too often we are actually blind to reality, whether it be in our relationships, how others perceive us, or our true spiritual condition before God. We are commanded to walk by faith and not by sight (2 Corinthians 5:7), and it's by hearing that we receive the Word, not by seeing (Romans 10:17).

All the way my Savior leads me

What have I to ask beside?
Can I doubt His faithful mercies?
Who through life has been my guide

Sheep are one of the most helpless creatures on earth, and are practically defenseless against predators. Sheep can even drown in shallow water because they are so helpless. Throughout the Scriptures people are compared to sheep, and as spiritual sheep who are prone to wander and slip into the pitfalls of life, we are in dire need of not just any shepherd, but the Good Shepherd. We need Him to protect us from our enemies and even from our own fallen nature. Though we may think we know the path that is best for us in this life, God personally knows each of us and the path He has mapped out for us. Our responsibility is to stop wandering aimlessly and follow Him wherever He may lead us.

As our Good Shepherd, He is loving, patient, merciful, and long-suffering towards us. Even when we blatantly rebel against Him and wander far from His path for us, He still seeks us out and draws us back to Him.

All of the way my Savior leads me
And He cheers each winding path I tread
Gives me strength for every trial
And He feeds me with the living bread

The picture of the Good Shepherd cheering us on and encouraging us through this life of trials is all too often prone to extremes in the modern church. On the one extreme, God is a wrathful judge waiting to zap us at the slightest infraction, while on the other, He's an old doting grandfather in whose eyes we can do no wrong regardless of our rebelliousness and sin. However, God is neither of those caricatures – He is holy, loving, and is committed to conforming us to Himself.

It isn't through life's pleasures that our faith grows and matures, but through life's trials. It is when we are broken and crushed that our true spiritual condition and utter dependence upon Him is revealed, and not only to others, but to ourselves. It is when we are lovingly though firmly chastised by our Father when His mercies are most clearly revealed to us.

And all the way my Savior leads me
  Oh, the fullness of His love
Perfect rest in me is promised
  In my Father's house above

Life is frequently wearisome and difficult, regardless of how much money, our good health, or how many creature-comforts we may have. How many millionaires or even billionaires are absolutely miserable and waste their fortunes on pleasures and toys in the vain attempt to find meaning in life? As mortal beings, our destiny is the grave.

Our life here in this world is one of toil, labor, and often meaninglessness, but very few ask why. If this life is all there really is, then why do we have such an internal sense of incompleteness? Could that be so we are nudged to seek after God and find our true fulfillment and complete rest in Him and Him alone? Someday we will be called Home, and then we will find complete peace and rest. But until then, we are to follow Him wherever He may lead us in the full assurance that He will bring us into that rest.

When my spirit clothed immortal
  Wings its flight through the realms of the day
This my song through endless ages
  Jesus led me all the way

What will our heart-song in Eternity be other than our praise to God for Who He is, all He has done for us, and His great, unfathomable love towards we who are often very unlovely? As lost sheep who are blind and completely dependent upon our Good Shepherd, only Jesus can lead us to our Heavenly Home.

2. Be With You

"When I was young, I was angry and I was kind of going, 'God, why am I such a freak? Why couldn't I have been a good basketball player? I wanted to be a jock or something. Instead I'm a musician. I feel like such a sissy all the time. Why couldn't I be just like a regular guy?' The more I thought about it, the more I realized that, you know, sometimes God has things in mind for us that we can't even imagine. And I think that maybe it was good for me to grow up being picked on a little bit, because then I realized what it meant to be kinda the underdog. And then to have someone who is not an underdog, someone like God, say, 'Hey, I want you to be with Me,' then you kinda go, 'Wow!' And so maybe for that reason, grace is more important to me than people who have been able to be more self-sufficient." – Rich Mullins

"Be With You" is one of those songs where Rich looks over his life from 20,000 feet and boils everything down to the fundamental meaning of life and our reason for existing: to be with God.

Throughout history, man has sought to determine what God expects of humankind. How can He be appeased? What can we do so that He blesses us, or at least not punish us? While God certainly wants justice, mercy, and order in our lives, His greatest desire from us is intimacy, a personal relationship between Him and the pinnacle of His creation.

What does any parent want most from their children? Sure, they typically want them to earn good grades in school, have a successful life, and usually produce grandkids, but deep down what do they want most? Intimacy – the same as in any marriage and most friendships. It's not even more time with their loved ones that people on their deathbeds really want as much as more intimacy.

Throughout the Old Testament, the Lord upholds one king above all the others who reigned, the man after His own heart regardless of how badly he messed up. In God's eyes, the greatest king in Israel/Judah wasn't the richest or wisest like Solomon, but the one who sought after Him with all his heart, his entire being: David. As the man who desired intimacy with God above all else, David the shepherd-king wrote the words of Psalm 27:4 – *"One thing I have desired of the Lord, that will I seek: That I may dwell in the house of the Lord all the days of my life, to behold the beauty of the Lord, and to inquire in His temple."* Not only is that David's heart-cry for God, but God's heart-cry for us – to dwell with us and be our God (Ezekiel 37:27, Revelation 21:3).

Stop for a moment and consider how mind-blowing that concept actually is: the All-Knowing, All-Powerful Creator of the universe wants to intimately know us and be intimately known by us who are mere scraps of clay and wisps of vapor. Our greatest desire should be to want to be with our Creator. Not only that, but consider that this intimacy (often through worship) is what He yearns for the most with us? How awesome is that?

In every relationship, intimacy is a two-way street. It's one thing to love another person, but it's something entirely different – something much, much greater – when that other person loves you back! True intimacy is to love AND be loved, and that's what God desires with each one of us. He loves us and wants us to reciprocate by loving Him in return and by loving those He has created. But does He ever force that intimacy? Of course not – if He did, then it wouldn't be love.

Be With You
<u>Phil 1:9-11; 2 Thess 1:3; Rev 6:12-14</u>

Everybody each and all
We're gonna die eventually
It's no more or less our faults
Than it is our destiny
So now Lord I come to you
Asking only for Your grace
You know what I've put myself through
All those empty dreams I chased

And when my body lies in the ruins
Of the lies that nearly ruined me
Will You pick up the pieces
That were pure and true
And breathe Your life into them
And set them free?

And when You start this world over
Again from scratch
Will You make me anew
Out of the stuff that lasts?
Stuff that's purer than gold is
And clearer than glass could ever be
Can I be with You?
Can I be with You?

And everybody all and each
From the day that we are born
We have to learn to walk beneath
Those mercies by which we're drawn

And now we wrestle in the dark
  With these angels that we can't see
We will move on although with scars
  Oh Lord, move inside of me

And when my body lies in the ruins
  Of the lies that nearly ruined me
Will You pick up the pieces
  That were pure and true
And breathe Your life into them
  And set them free?

And when You blast this cosmos
  To kingdom come
When those jagged-edged mountains
  I love are gone
When the sky is crossed with the tears
  Of a thousand falling suns
As they crash into the sea
  Can I be with you?
Can I be with you?

As I survey modern Christendom and much of church history over the last two thousand years, I contend that many people become Christians for the wrong reasons, namely for fire-insurance. The fear of going to Hell brings many to repentance, the same as many wanting to go to Heaven. But is that really what the Gospel is all about, avoiding Hell and getting a free-pass into Heaven? Not at all – the heart of the Gospel is intimacy with God through His Son Jesus Christ and having the Holy Spirit indwell us. But because we are fallen and sinful, accepting the forgiveness and the new life He offers is the ONLY way to approach Him and have intimacy with Him.

Hell isn't merely a punishment for those who reject God as much as the logical consequence of their choice to not be with Him, their rejection of not only Him, but His Providence for them. Imagine having a child who grows up and wants nothing at all to do with you. Though you loved them, raised them, and sacrificed your all for them, they don't want to even speak with you, much less live with you. The same is true with many who reject God, except that His house is all of Creation. Where else can they go except into the Outer Darkness, as far away from His Presence as possible?

Yes, God doesn't want anyone to perish, but what He really wants is intimacy with us. And that intimacy is infinitely greater and better than fire-insurance.

Everybody each and all
 We're gonna die eventually
It's no more or less our faults
 Than it is our destiny
So now Lord I come to you
 Asking only for Your grace
You know what I've put myself through
 All those empty dreams I chased

The greatest tragedy since the Fall of Man in the Garden of Eden is Death, which when properly put in perspective makes much of life utterly meaningless. We are born, we live for a blip of time, and then we die and return to the dust. Everything and everyone that we have loved, dreamed about, toiled over, and lived for passes away into nothingness. When you think about it, the reality of death makes much of life completely pointless. As mortal creatures, death is our ultimate destination – unless death is not really the end.

For much of the Old Testament, Sheol was the soul's destination after death, but when Jesus came, He revealed that there is much more to the afterlife. Sheol is not our ultimate destination, but either Heaven (where God's throne is) or Hell (the Outer Darkness). The Good News – the Gospel – that Jesus proclaimed is that we have a choice: we can believe in Him and receive the eternal life that He offers, or we can continue on the Highway to Hell, the default destination for fallen mankind.

It is only through God's unfathomable love and grace towards us that we have the incredible opportunity to receive the eternal life that He – and He alone – can offer. And the life He offers isn't merely a "Get Out of Hell" card or a "Get Into Heaven" pass, but adoption as sons and daughters of God Himself! Romans 8:16-17 says that *"The Spirit Himself bears witness with our spirit that we are children of God, and if children, then heirs – heirs of God and joint heirs with Christ, if indeed we suffer with Him, that we may also be glorified together."*

When we accept Christ, we not only become citizens of Heaven but fellow heirs with Him!

And when my body lies in the ruins
Of the lies that nearly ruined me
Will You pick up the pieces
That were pure and true
And breathe Your life into them
And set them free?

When the day comes and we finally die (the Rapture excluded), when the wood, hay, and stubble of our lives has been sifted through and burned away, what will remain of us? All those miles we ran, the years spent in the gym, and the tons of organic food we ate won't amount to a hill of beans. All that will remain is our faith and the love that we gave God and others. Everything else is temporary, immaterial, and meaningless in the grand scheme of things.

Love is all that will last of us when everything else is purged away. The Bible speaks of two judgment seats each of us will face: the Bema Seat or the White Throne, the difference being that the former is for the Saved and the latter is for the Lost. After death, believers in Christ will stand before the Bema Seat or the Throne of Rewards and face the King. This is a judgment of works, or rather, an awards ceremony – it is a place to commend rather than condemn as with the White Throne Judgment.

Some will receive many crowns and commendations at the Bema Seat, while many will sadly not. Those at the Bema Seat Judgment are given new bodies fitting for our new service to Christ, according to what we did here on earth before. Those who were faithful with their earthly service will be given much more honor and responsibilities in their eternal service (Matthew 25:14-30). Our faithfulness, personal integrity, purity, sacrifice, and love will be what determine our heavenly rewards.

We will ALL stand before Christ one day and give an accounting for ourselves and what we have done for this blip of time we call "life" – but whether we are commended or condemned is up to us. What will remain of us after everything is burned away? Only the pieces that were pure and true – how we loved others and how we walked in this world.

And when You start this world over
   Again from scratch
Will You make me anew
   Out of the stuff that lasts?
Stuff that's purer than gold is
   And clearer than glass could ever be
Can I be with You?
   Can I be with You?

Most people believe – especially the vast majority of Christians – is that Heaven is our final destination, but that is only partially true. According to the book of Isaiah and Revelation, after the Millennium (the literal 1000-year reign of Christ upon the Earth), God will release His hold on Creation and everything – time, space, and matter – will be destroyed. But then He will make the new heavens and the new earth, those which will last for all eternity. Once Creation has been remade, the New Jerusalem (or Heaven) will descend to earth and God will dwell with us. We Christians will only be away from earth in Heaven for a rather short time, though we will still be in Heaven. God brings Heaven to Earth to dwell among us.

The last two verses of this song proclaim Rich's heart-cry, which should be that of everyone but especially those who are called by His name: *"Can I be with you?"* Consider that again for a moment – God, the Eternal Creator of the Universe – wants to be with us! The very idea that God would even want to look at us in our fallen, broken condition is shockingly unfathomable. And all He really wants from us in return is for us to want to be with Him!

When the sky is crossed with the tears
  Of a thousand falling suns
As they crash into the sea
  Can I be with you?
Can I be with you?

The song ends with some of the most dramatic prose in all of Rich's songs: *"When the sky is crossed with the tears of a thousand falling suns as they crash into the sea."* I can almost picture that scene now as we stand upon the Crystal Sea before Christ and watch in awe and wonder as He remakes the universe from scratch.

3. Both Feet on the Ground

"You will be lonely for a good part of your life, so just get used to it. Remember, someday you'll be dead. It won't last forever. So while you still have life, love everybody you can love. Love them as much as you can love them. Don't try to keep them for yourself. Because when you're gone, they'll just resent you for having left. Love freely." – Rich Mullins

"Both Feet on the Ground" is one of the all-but-forgotten songs on Rich's first album with a gentle beat and slower rhythm. Some of his first songs were rather raw and cutting, like "Elijah" and "A Few Good Men," but not this one. It has a waltzy or even a slow two-step feel, and I only discovered this song within the last few years as I started learning to dance.

While the song is mostly about being in love, it's more about being steady and sure in Christ even though it seems like everyone around you is in love with someone else. It's one thing to be alone, but quite another to be lonely, particularly when it feels like you're the only one who feels that way. Loneliness is probably the most acute when you're out somewhere and it seems like everyone has someone – except you.

For those of us who seek to walk with God, we're never really alone, and the love that He gives us is the one with both feet on the ground – the love that will last for eternity.

Both Feet on the Ground
1 John 4:16

They pass two by two, star-dazed
They gaze at the lights on the avenue
Just like when love is new
It's Saturday night and I know that they think I'm alone
Oh but I'm alright
I got You by my side

And I'm not head over heels, and I'm not on cloud nine
And I don't think love is blind
'Cause I know that You see me and yet
You still choose to be mine
With a love that will stand even when I fall down
I know You'll pick me up somehow
And You say that to love is to love
With both feet on the ground

Passing by, they glide on the music
As free as two birds in flight
At least they are tonight
But I'm just out of reach of the lights
And the music the silence out
On the beach
I know that's where we'll meet

And I'm not head over heels, and I'm not on cloud nine
And I don't think love is blind
'Cause I know that You see me and yet
You still choose to be mine
With a love that will stand even when I fall down
I know You'll pick me up somehow
And You say that to love is to love
With both feet on the ground

When two people are in love, it's amazingly easy and effortless to be swept away by all the intense emotions and experience unbelievable highs and heart-wrenching lows. Those incredible feelings are a big part of what makes being in love feel so ecstatic and wonderful. Remember what that's like: your heart pounds furiously, you can barely breathe, and romantic songs start playing inside your head.

However, most people will be in love for only a short period of their lives. Even married couples may truly feel "in love" for only a few years before the familiarity and pressures of life creep in and dampen those feelings. Many couples love one another but are no longer "in love" with one another.

The main message of this song is that the best love is being in love with God and having a steady, consistent relationship with Him and not being swept away by all these highs and lows as in human romantic relationships that are swirling all around us. It's not that those emotions and experiences are bad as much as that they're often fleeting and temporary. Many people are simply in love with being in love – like alcohol, drugs, or other highs.

I remember the first time I really connected with God and finally turned my life over to Him – I can still picture it and almost even feel it as if it happened only yesterday. When I was about a year out of high school, I had the opportunity to live very close to the beach in Cape Canaveral, Florida for about six months. I was sitting on my surfboard a hundred feet or so off the shoreline when He finally broke through to me. The swells were few that night, and as I was waiting for the next one to come in, I finally started asking the right questions and sought Him. And He was finally able to reach my heart.

Before I knew it, there I was alone with the waves with tears streaming down my cheeks, falling in love with God. For a few days afterward, there was a sweetness, fervor, and intensity that I had never experienced before. But over the weeks and months that followed, those feelings gradually lessened and I settled into a steady, growing relationship with Him.

The same holds true with most couples: they meet, get to know each other a little, and if the chemistry is right (or the moon is full), they fall in love and get swept away for a while. If the feelings and chemistry are deep enough, the relationship becomes more permanent. But sooner or later, the high-octane feelings begin to lessen and genuine, real love begins to grow and replace those initial intense emotions.

They pass two by two, star-dazed
They gaze at the lights on the avenue
Just like when love is new
It's Saturday night and I know that they think I'm alone
Oh but I'm alright
I got You by my side

Each time I hear this verse, I remember walking along the boardwalk in Tel Aviv during my first tour of Israel in 2010. It was our first night there and my first time seeing the Mediterranean Sea. Not only that, but it was Saturday night just after Shabbat had ended and all the shops and restaurants were lit up and couples were walking arm-in-arm enjoying the sights. Meanwhile, I'm by myself and taking in all the sights I possibly can. Yet later that night, I couldn't help but think of the happy couples and what they must've thought of me, this goofy American walking alone with a awestruck look on my face.

That begs the question, "If God is with us, are we really alone?" Most assuredly not, though it may often feel that way! As I'm adjusting to my new life, yes, there are often dark periods of loneliness, particularly in the middle of the night. But even then God is with me (Psalm 139) – I couldn't escape His Presence even if I tried! God is there whether I can see Him or not, whether I can hear Him or not, and even if I can't feel Him or not. Since Jesus lived as a bachelor for His entire life (though most men in that culture were married by their late teens), He has experienced similar times of intense loneliness. However, He never let them define Him or conquer Him.

What a comfort it is to know that God can relate to us wherever we may be, that He has felt what we feel and has struggled with the same sorrows and hardships that we do (and then some!). He knows just how heavy our hearts can be and how bitterly we grieve and even languish in our loneliness.

And I'm not head over heels, and I'm not on cloud nine
And I don't think love is blind
'Cause I know that You see me and yet
You still choose to be mine
With a love that will stand even when I fall down
I know You'll pick me up somehow
And You say that to love is to love
With both feet on the ground

The chorus holds the key to the entire song: that real love isn't blind, and that real love doesn't roll in and out with the waves. Very often in romantic relationships, love really is blind, or rather, we are blinded by our emotions and desires, our own personal fairy tales. To our detriment, we sometimes see only what we choose to see, and not see things as they really are. Sometimes, we even have this notion that the warning signs aren't really as bad as they seem because we want that relationship to continue and progress. I know that firsthand from my own marriage and prior relationships.

I love the phrase *"Cause I know that you see me and yet you still choose to be mine"* – it literally brings a smile to my

31

face every time I hear it. That wonderful idea of completely belonging to someone, that you are theirs and that they are yours exclusively, that you see one another for who you both really are and you still love one another despite your flaws, differences, and stumblings. It's that unconditional acceptance that we so often crave, yet seldom find – but with God, it's always there. He always accepts us – and He proved it by sending His Son to take our infirmities and punishment upon Himself.

If we really want to know what real love is, we should simply ask the Author of love. What is real love from God's point of view? Love is best defined in 1 Corinthians 13 4-8a: *"Love suffers long and is kind; love does not envy; love does not parade itself, is not puffed up; does not behave rudely, does not seek its own, is not provoked, thinks no evil; does not rejoice in iniquity, but rejoices in the truth; bears all things, believes all things, hopes all things, endures all things. Love never fails."* It is this love that endures long after the romantic, puppy-dog love has faded away.

Real love is like a thick slab of granite. Nothing will break it, and nothing will crush it. Even when there are failures and set-backs, scratches and chips in it, real love endures. In a good marriage or a good family, real love suffers and forgives; real love picks that other person back up when they fall down. Real love seeks to heal what is hurt and bind up what is broken.

Romantic love takes time to settle out and steady itself. One of the big mistakes in many marriages (including my own) is that couples rush into dating, engagement, and marriage much too fast. For us, we were high on love (and the idea of love) and we wanted that high to keep going up and up and up. We were both immature and impatient and wanted to marry a decent, attractive Christian, have a Christian marriage, and build a Christian family. But it didn't work out quite that way in the end.

The fundamental problem before we entered the marriage covenant was that we didn't really stop and ask ourselves if this was the person we really wanted to spend the rest of our lives with before we stood before the altar. If we would have slowed down and observed one another and had "both feet on the ground" for a while, perhaps it wouldn't have progressed to marriage and then ended as it did.

So what should real love look like in a relationship? Though I did not really experience it in much of my marriage, I have some thoughts from the Scriptures and other books about what it should be. Real love is about growing in intimacy and closeness with that one other special person, the melding of two hearts and souls into one. It's not merely the romantic, ooey-gooey stuff of mush that Hollywood loves to mass-market, though that is nice to keep the spark in the relationship. Real love is much, much greater than romantic love, which can often be fleeting and turbulent. Real love is the type of love that bears all things, believes all things, trusts all things, and hopes all things – the love that can heal badly wounded people and mend terribly broken hearts.

Real love is that which God has for us and what He hopes we have towards Him. How mind-blowing it is that God not only wants us to be with Him, but that He wants to be with us! Think about that for a moment – God sees us not only at our best, but at our very worst and every humdrum moment in between. Would you want to be with a flea or a worm, a fallen creature of the dust? Probably not – yet God wants to be with us despite our frequent tantrums and sinfulness! And He doesn't want to be with us for just a few moments, He wants to be with us for all eternity!

Passing by, they glide on the music
As free as two birds in flight
At least they are tonight
But I'm just out of reach of the lights

And the music the silence out
  On the beach
I know that's where we'll meet

When I lived in Cape Canaveral, one of my favorite activities was to walk the beach, which I did nearly every evening after work and for several hours on the weekends. The night-walks on the beach – especially when the moon was bright and haloed – were the best! The sand, surf, and sun were much different from the fields of corn, wheat, and soybeans that I had been surrounded with in Ohio, and I simply couldn't get enough of it.

This verse always brings to mind the sea gulls gliding effortlessly on the ocean breeze and soaring back and forth before landing to scavenge or beg. The Cocoa Beach Pier is nearby with the reggae music playing and the lights of the condos and beach-houses twinkling along the shore. Meanwhile, I'm walking by the pulsing waves getting to know my Maker for the first time in my life. Of all the times I've spoken with God and walked with Him, those solitary moments are among the most precious. Though to everyone else I was all alone, He was right by my side.

It was on those beaches in and by those endless waves that I first really walked with Him and surrendered my life to Him. God took this broken, screwed-up mess of a life I was making for myself and saved me from it. He kept pursuing me despite how long and how far I had tried to run away from Him. That is real love – the love that waits. The love that redeems. The love that saves.

4. Boy Like Me / Man Like You

"I grew up hearing everyone tell me 'God loves you'. I would say big deal – God loves everybody. That don't make me special! That just proves that God ain't got no taste. And, I don't think He does. Thank God! Because He takes the junk of our lives and makes the most beautiful art." – Rich Mullins

The song "Boy Like Me / Man Like You" is one of Rich's more lighthearted works, in which he compares his boyhood years to those of Jesus. What was He really like, especially in His younger years? The Bible says very little about most of His life, and it's often easy to think of Him only as an infant or a grown man. There is the passage in Luke 2 which tells of the time when He stayed behind in Jerusalem and wowed the Pharisees at the Temple, but that's about it.

What was Jesus like as a boy growing up in Nazareth? Did He play the same silly childhood games that most kids do? Did He ever chase His brothers and sisters or kick a ball around with the other neighborhood kids? Did He have a puppy that would follow Him all over the place and share in His boyhood adventures? Did He cry over that same dog and hug him one more time as he took his final breath?

Did He feel shy when girls looked at Him funny or giggled at Him when He hit puberty and His voice cracked and His face got all pimply? How did He feel when He was an adolescent and His ears, hands, or feet were no longer in proportion to the rest of His growing body? Did His face ever turn bright red when He realized the neighborhood girls were whispering about Him? Did He ever have a crush on any of them (or they on Him), and did He ever get passed a love-note in class?

From Hebrews 4, we know that Jesus was tempted in every way that we are, but He remained sinless. I would say that He experienced many of the same things we all did when we were growing up, though of course the era and culture was much different.

Boy Like Me / Man Like You
Matthew 2:21-23, Luke 2:39-52, Colossians 1:9-14, 2:6-10

You was a baby like I was once
*   You was cryin' in the early mornin'*
You was born in a stable Lord
*   Reid Memorial is where I was born*
They wrapped You in swaddling clothes
*   Me they dressed in baby blue*

But I was twelve years old in the meeting house
*   Listening to the old men pray*
And I was tryin' hard to figure out
*   What it was that they was tryin' to say*
There You were in the temple
*   They said You weren't old enough*
To know the things You knew

Well, did You grow up hungry?
*   Did You grow up fast?*
Did the little girls giggle when You walked past?
*   Did You wonder what it was that made them laugh?*
And did they tell You stories 'bout the saints of old?
*   Stories about their faith?*
They say stories like that make a boy grow bold

Stories like that make a man walk straight

And You was a boy like I was once
   But was You a boy like me
Well, I grew up around Indiana
   You grew up around Galilee
And if I ever really do grow up
   Lord I want to grow up and be just like You

Well, did You wrestle with a dog and lick his nose?
   Did You play beneath the spray of a water hose?
Did You ever make angels in the winter snow?
   And did they tell You stories 'bout the saints of old?
Stories about their faith?
   They say stories like that make a boy grow bold
Stories like that make a man walk straight

Did You ever get scared playing hide and seek?
   Did You try not to cry when You scraped Your knee?
Did You ever skip a rock across a quiet creek?
   And did they tell You stories 'bout the saints of old?
Stories about their faith?
   They say stories like that make a boy grow bold
Stories like that make a man walk straight

And I really may just grow up and be like You someday

Along with "First Family," this song is one of those that I can easily relate to, mostly because of where Rich grew up and his home-life out in the country. While he was born and raised on a farm in central-eastern Indiana, I grew up on one in northwestern Ohio in the very corner of the state, sometimes known as the "armpit" because of the borders and because it used to be the Black Swamp before being drained about a century ago.

Back home, our two-acre plot was surrounded by fields and woods, though none of them were ours. We had all sorts of fruit trees and several large gardens where we grew strawberries, potatoes, and a variety of produce. If it could be grown in Ohio, it could probably found somewhere on our property. Mom would can or freeze most of what we grew, and when we had too much we would sell it or give it away. When we weren't slaving away roto-tilling, planting, hoeing, weeding, pruning, or picking, we would be chopping, throwing, or stacking wood for the winter. When I was older, I usually mowed most of the yard, including the rhubarb patch by the barn so I wouldn't have to eat it later as pie. (Sorry Mom, but if it looks like weeds and tastes like weeds...) I don't remember ever wearing shirts in the summer except on Sundays and when our grandparents came over.

While my two brothers and I loathed most of the work we had to do, it kept us out of a lot of the trouble we probably would've gotten into, though we constantly complained and had more than our fair share of fights and spankings. But looking back now, all that sweat and hard work was worth it – our parents gave us a love for the outdoors, for growing things, and not being afraid of hard work.

The work-ethic that growing up in the country produced has served me well for most of my life. My first real paid job was bailing hay for the neighbors and helping with one of the horse-farms down the road. We couldn't afford horses of our own, so I had to make due with getting my horse-fix in with the neighbors'. Now that I've worked in an office-setting since college, working outside is often a welcome relief – well, almost!

One of the more memorable times back home was when I took up running in high school and would run by the pastures. I would usually put in a couple miles in the evenings after the chores were finished, just about the time when the neighbor's cows would be ready to head in for the night. One night while I was running by, I heard them all start mooing and noticed the entire herd trotting after me. Low and behold, somehow I had unwittingly become a cattle rustler each night I went running, which unfortunately continued until I left home. So much for trying to impress any girls that happened to be driving by!

From a young age, Rich's heart-cry was to be like Jesus, and you can be sure he thought of Him quite often while he was doing his chores on the farm and long after he left home, which came out in his songs. Some of his funnier stories are when he got all four tractor tires stuck in the holes they were digging for trees, and when a tractor wheel fell off. Most farm work is monotonous and boring, and there's lots of time to think about God when you're plowing the fields, milking the cows, or even just mowing the lawn.

The closing verse of the chorus is about making "boys grow bold" and "men walk straight" – in essence, transforming boys into men. What really makes us grow up? What really turns boys into men?

Today in our era of man-children (or adult boys), it's often easier to see what does not make a boy into a man than what does. Is it by growing taller, stronger, and smarter the cause for the transformation? Definitely not. Is it by getting a college degree (of any flavor), working hard, or building a career? Not usually. Does having a lot of money and financial smarts mature young men? Nope – that just provides more money for their toys (or girlfriends). What about serving in the armed forces? Not always. What about having a beautiful girlfriend, being engaged, or even getting married? Sometimes, but there are many married boys out there. Does having a couple of kids do the trick? Not necessarily, but that's getting closer to the mark.

What turns boys into men is when they take responsibility for themselves, keep their word/promises, and make personal sacrifices for the benefit of others – regardless of what it may cost them personally. Typically this transformation is caused by the needs of their wife and children, but also their parents and others who may need their attention, time, and strength. The making of a man involves heavy doses of personal self-control, humility, integrity, faithfulness, patience, purity, and a lot of sacrifice. Real men give of themselves and pour themselves out for the betterment of those around them. Real men accept responsibility for their families and loved ones regardless of their own personal happiness and fulfillment. Real men sacrifice and count it all joy.

The Bible is full of the profiles of different men across a wide spectrum of personalities, cultures, and temperaments. Some were brave and strong, while others were wafflers and cowards. The men I view as personal role-models in the Bible are usually Job, David, Daniel, Paul, and of course, Jesus. The traits that all of them have in common are a deep love of God, the utmost devotion to His Word, an intimate prayer life, incredible personal integrity and purity (usually), and making very difficult personal sacrifices in order to be faithful to God.

If we are to be men and women of God, then we must cultivate a deep, daily relationship with Him and His Word, and to not only read or hear it, but actually obey it and DO it – regardless of the cost.

5. The Breaks

"It's kind of like the apostle Paul's thing about losing your life to find it. Growing up in the 60's and 70's, people said 'I'm going out to find myself.' And it's sort of silly. My parents would say, 'How did they lose themselves?'... And so in the process of living, and trying to be faithful to Christ but not doctrinally narrow, I'm asking [in the song "The Breaks"] that if I were to hold on to Christ, what would that be, and what would that not be? And in light of that, let me let go, oh God, in your mercy, of everything that is not you."
– Rich Mullins

In the America today, so much of life seems to be about chasing after our dreams and things we think we want, stuff that we hope will bring us happiness or fulfillment, only to find that they fall painfully short soon after we obtain them. In my own experience as a writer, I've noticed that whenever I finish a book, I feel a mixture of relief about achieving my goal and yet also a certain sadness that it's finally over, as if I'm left wondering, "Great! So what am I supposed to do now?" As Solomon himself once said, "Of making many books there is no end, and much study is wearisome to the flesh." (Ecclesiastes 12:12) No kidding!

One of the undeniable truths of life is that we become like whatever we pour ourselves into, the idols we prostrate ourselves before, like our hobbies and careers and entertainments. In short, we become like the gods we worship. So with that in mind, shouldn't we be very careful

41

about how we spend our time and energy and what we pour ourselves into? If we try to seize life by the horns and achieve all that we can, will that really fulfill us? No – true meaning and contentment is found when we pour ourselves out like a drink-offering on God's altar of the broken world around us.

"The Breaks" is about giving ourselves away in order to find lasting peace and fulfillment, of laying up those little treasures in Heaven which will never be taken away from us, instead of clinging to the fleeting, worthless treasures of earth. This is one of those songs I like to listen to when I find myself losing perspective or get disappointed over something I really shouldn't.

The Breaks
1 Cor 9:24-27

Here is my heart take what you want
'Cause I have no use for it anyway
Well of all the stupid things I've ever said
This could be the worst may be the best
But those are the breaks
These are the bruises
And if I can't give myself away
I'm the only one who loses
And I don't want to lose this

It is the sea that makes the sailor
And the land that shapes the sea
And I do not know yet what I am made of
Or all I may someday be
And it is the wood that makes a carpenter
It's the very tools of his trade
And it is love that makes a lover
And a cross that makes a saint

Here is my song, listen if you will
But I have no heart for it anymore
I just have half a mind to cut it loose
And if it sails off into the blue
Then I'll just let it soar
And the sky is better keeping
And I won't be any poorer
For giving it its freedom
And here's one for freedom

It is the sea that makes the sailor
And the land that shapes the sea
And I do not know yet what I am made of
Or all I may someday be
It is the wood that makes a carpenter
It's the very tools of his trade
And it is love that makes a lover
And a cross that makes a saint

Well, of all the stupid things I've ever said
This could be the worst may be the best
But those are the breaks

Though we may only live for a few decades in this world, a mere blip in the span of eternity, life still has a way of becoming rather wearisome and meaningless. Even those who are just entering adulthood can sense life's vanity and pointlessness all too often.

Life can appear quite meaningless if we focus only on the goals, possessions, and achievements that we obtain along the way, which soon fade and pass into obscurity. But what if life is more about the journey itself rather than reaching the destination? What if the true significance of life is found in how well we love along the way, the lives we touch, and the people we become? With that perspective, the road of life suddenly doesn't seem nearly so pointless and wearisome, does it?

Along life's journey, we fallen creatures say countless stupid words and do endless stupid things. We make mistake after mistake and falter time and time again. But that's life in this world of sin and brokenness. We can fight it and rage against it all we want, but that won't change much of anything. From Romans 8:28, we know that all things work together for good to those who love God. Not some things, but ALL things – our breaks, our bruises, our screw-ups, and everything in between.

Here is my heart take what you want
'Cause I have no use for it anyway
Well of all the stupid things I've ever said
This could be the worst may be the best
But those are the breaks
These are the bruises
And if I can't give myself away
I'm the only one who loses
And I don't want to lose this

What does God want most from us? It's not our time, money, or service that He really desires – He wants our hearts, our intimacy with Him. It is in the realm of the heart that God seeks to operate in us, making a new man destined for eternity from the ashes of the old one already destined for death. Often He uses a thin scalpel as during a delicate, complicated surgery, but other times He wields a bone-saw to cut away bone, sinew, and flesh. He has freely given Himself to us in that we might turn and freely give ourselves back to Him, along with pouring ourselves out to one another.

Jesus poured Himself out to us to give us His life – how can we possibly expect to not do likewise if we are to be remade in His image? We in the Church are referred to as the Body of Christ, and I'm pretty sure He wasn't just using a clever metaphor. If He as the Head sacrificed and suffered, then we as the Body should expect to sacrifice and suffer also.

When our puff of time here on earth is over, God isn't going to ask about how well we've preserved that rotted corpse we dwelled in for a few years down here – He's going to ask whether we put that body to good use with the time we were given. Anyone who doesn't arrive in Heaven with some bruises, breaks, and battle-scars probably didn't do very much to further His Kingdom. He wants us bruised, beaten-up, and broken, because that means we were living and growing in Him.

Does that mean we're only useful to Him on some distant mission-field living among head-hunters? No – our mission-field is wherever we happen to find ourselves in life. Our mission-field is to everyone around us as we go through life in this broken world. He wants us to live for Him and pour ourselves out like drink-offerings, as living sacrifices. Parents and caretakers regularly give themselves away and pour themselves into those in their care, and how well they do that makes all the difference. If we can't give ourselves away, then we really are the ones who lose, and not only at the end of our lives.

In Israel, the Jewish people have an unofficial mission statement called "tikkun olam" which means "repairing the world." What a beautiful picture of how we should serve those around us and what we should have as our purpose in this life. If we really want to heal the world, we need to give ourselves away and pour ourselves into those around us.

It is the sea that makes the sailor
And the land that shapes the sea
And I do not know yet what I am made of
Or all I may someday be

And it is the wood that makes a carpenter
It's the very tools of his trade
And it is love that makes a lover
And a cross that makes a saint

The furniture and crafts a carpenter produces are often only as good as the wood he used. After all, there isn't much he can do with a board that's full of cracks and knots and rot. The reputation of the carpenter is only as good as the wood he chooses to work with before he begins to fashion it. Perhaps that's a good analogy as to why God in His sovereignty chooses some to be in His Kingdom but not others, even though everyone is invited. But the funny thing about God is that He tends to use the weak, broken, and knotted people in His Kingdom the most (1 Corinthians 1:26-29). It's the character of the wood He is most concerned with, not just how it looks on the outside. He is more concerned with who He truly can mold and shape for his purposes than our various accomplishments.

The same is true with a sailor. The sailor in the middle of a hurricane in the Caribbean is much different than the sailor on a glassy lake. Just as the ferocity and trials of the sea make the sailor into who he is, so the Cross shapes and molds us into instruments for Christ. Following Him and bearing our crosses relentlessly through life is what turns sinners into saints through sanctification. It's not meant to be pleasant like that silly health-n-wealth gospel peddled around today. This journey of life is about conforming us to the image of Christ and His likeness, not merely to reach the final destination of Heaven.

Bearing our crosses means shouldering that terrible burden we can barely even lift at times and dragging ourselves along through the jeering crowds with that beam on our backs. It's in the suffering and brokenness that we are conformed to Him, our daily dying to ourselves that refines and reshapes our souls and conforms us to His likeness.

6. Calling Out Your Name

"The longer I live, the more I have the feeling like God looks down, like when you've just bitten into a vanilla ice cream cone, you just get the feeling God's going, 'Yes! He enjoys it, and I made his taste buds and I made vanilla and he's putting it together and he's experiencing what I created him to experience.'" – Rich Mullins

"Calling Out Your Name" is one of those songs that always puts a gleam in my eye. The song begins with Rich slowly striking the strings on his hammered dulcimer and then he picks up the tempo and hammers away at it for the rest of the piece. It was this song that inspired me to construct my own hammered dulcimer soon after I heard it years ago, though I must confess that I haven't learned to play it well at all. But it's on my bucket-list and I'll get around to it someday, probably after relearning how to play the piano after 30+ years (Mrs. Stuckey would be so proud!).

This song proclaims the wonders and beauty of God's creation in the poetic prose that Rich was renowned for, particularly in the American "fly-over" country that is all-too-often ignored or overlooked today.

Calling Out Your Name
Psalm 19:1-6; Psalm 65:5-13

Well the moon moved past Nebraska

And spilled laughter on them cold Dakota Hills
And angels danced on Jacob's stairs
Yeah, they danced on Jacob's stairs
There is this silence in the Badlands
And over Kansas the whole universe was stilled
By the whisper of a prayer
The whisper of a prayer

And the single hawk bursts into flight
And in the east the whole horizon is in flames
I feel thunder in the sky
I see the sky about to rain
And I hear the prairies calling out Your name

I can feel the earth tremble
Beneath the rumbling of the buffalo hooves
And the fury in the pheasant's wings
And there's fury in a pheasant's wings
It tells me the Lord is in His temple
And there is still a faith that can make the mountains move
And a love that can make the heavens ring
And I've seen love make heaven ring

Where the sacred rivers meet
Beneath the shadow of the Keeper of the plains
I feel thunder in the sky
I see the sky about to rain
And I hear the prairies calling out Your name

From the place where morning gathers
You can look sometimes forever 'til you see
What time may never know
What time may never know
How the Lord takes by its corners this old world
And shakes us forward and shakes us free

To run wild with the hope
To run wild with the hope

The hope that this thirst will not last long
That it will soon drown in the song not sung in vain
And I feel thunder in the sky
I see the sky about to rain
And I hear the prairies calling out Your name

And I know this thirst will not last long
That it will soon drown in the song not sung in vain
I feel thunder in the sky
I see the sky about to rain
And with the prairies I am calling out Your name

God made this incredible world for us to explore and enjoy, to reveal Himself and His attributes to us, and to show us who He is and what He loves. As more of the world becomes urbanized, the incredible handiwork of God is replaced by the profane, ugly handiwork of men. Is God best seen in a concrete jungle or in a real jungle? Can God be best heard in a city full of honking horns or in the lonely cry of an eagle as it soars high above the prairie?

One of the greatest passages about the Creation is not found in Genesis, but in the latter chapters of the book of Job (38-40). After Job and his friends have finished exchanging barbs and opinions about the character of God, the Lord Himself grants Job an audience with Him. But rather than answering Job's questions about why he's been suffering so badly, God goes into meticulous detail about how He watches over everything He has made and cares for it every moment of every day. The tiniest details we would view as insignificant are not insignificant to Him at all! As He so often does with us, God did answer Job's questions and prayers, but not in the way he had expected (or hoped!).

After God created the world and rested on the Seventh Day, He didn't just set everything in motion, dust off His hands, and then move on to another project; He is intimately involved in every aspect of His creation and cares for it moment by moment.

Well the moon moved past Nebraska
  And spilled laughter on them cold Dakota Hills
And angels danced on Jacob's stairs
  Yeah, they danced on Jacob's stairs
There is this silence in the Badlands
  And over Kansas the whole universe was stilled
By the whisper of a prayer
  The whisper of a prayer

One of the items on my personal bucket-list is to ride a motorcycle through the Badlands of South Dakota, primarily thanks to this song. The vast, rugged wilderness of the Badlands and the crystal-clear night sky proclaim the wonders of God's handiwork: the stars and constellations! Though the Information Age, supersonic travel, and urbanization have made the world seem rather small, God made it to be big and wonderful and mysterious. And if we want to make the world feel big again, we need to get away from all the distractions and the artificial world we've constructed.

God has this incredible ability to scatter a fistful of dust in the air and make a breathtaking sunset, and take a bunch of broken rocks and rubble and create wonders like the Grand Canyon and the Badlands. And how does God want us to respond to such wonders? With wordless awe and appreciation at His handiwork.

And the single hawk bursts into flight
  And in the east the whole horizon is in flames
I feel thunder in the sky

I see the sky about to rain
And I hear the prairies calling out Your name

The chorus is a great example of how Rich could paint majestic, resonating pictures with a handful of words. Close your eyes and imagine the scene of the flying hawk as it furiously rushes to meet the dawn that's setting the eastern sky in flames. Listen to the rumbling thunder in the distance and sniff that peculiar smell in the air just before the clouds are about to burst open with rain. Though the prairies may be overlooked and ignored by many today, that still, small voice of our Creator can still be heard on the wind rustling in the plains and the tall grasses.

Names are funny things at times; they can communicate family, lineage, reputation, authority, identity, purpose, and even personality. Just the mere mention of some names can strike fear in the bravest of people. I've never been all that crazy about my name, particularly my last name since everyone spells it with the Americanized version of "Hamilton" thanks to the guy on the $10 bill and the others who took the easy way out in spelling our family name from the southern part of England. As a school teacher, my dad had a clever way of teaching it to his students, but that's another story – let's just say that they never forgot it.

God is referred to by more than a dozen names throughout the Bible such as Adonai, Yahweh (and all its variations), Elohim, El Shaddai, and others. God's Name is highly honored throughout the Scriptures, but what does He honor even above His Name and His reputation? Psalm 138:2 says that He has magnified His Word – the Scriptures that too often sit collecting dust on our bookshelves – above His Name! How different our homes, churches, schools, neighborhoods, and country would be if we really honored God by reading His Word and actually following it?

I can feel the earth tremble

Beneath the rumbling of the buffalo hooves
And the fury in the pheasant's wings
   And there's fury in a pheasant's wings
It tells me the Lord is in His temple
   And there is still a faith that can make the mountains move
And a love that can make the heavens ring
   And I've seen love make heaven ring

Though I've lived in Colorado for the last fifteen years, I have only seen a handful of buffalo. The plains used to teem with them until more a century ago when the Native Americans and settlers (and railroads) pushed west too fast and all but exterminated them. Today, there are pockets of buffalo in Yosemite and in other parts of the West, but they will never return to their vast numbers. Imagine what the plains used to sound like when millions of buffalo roamed free and would thunder across the prairie? I'm sure the prairie-dogs weren't too thrilled about it, but neighbors are neighbors.

Even though we may think that we've supplanted God in this modern, sophisticated world, we have not. With sophistication and technology comes increasing fragility and complexity. Though we have all these incredible wonders to make our lives easier, we have become so specialized and dependent on these conveniences that most people would have a very difficult time functioning if these conveniences were suddenly yanked away – myself included!

Though America is humming along with all these modern conveniences (running water, electricity, cars, computers, Internet), consider that it all hinges upon the steady flow of electricity. Now consider that just a handful of nuclear bombs detonated over the continent could easily knock out the entire power-grid and plunge us back to the Nineteenth Century in seconds. It isn't a nuclear attack that would decimate the country but an EMP (electromagnetic pulse) attack, which is what several of our enemies have been training for. There is no known defense for an EMP other than being prepared with an ample supply of food and water (and ammunition!).

From the place where morning gathers
*   You can look sometimes forever 'til you see*
What time may never know
*   What time may never know*
How the Lord takes by its corners this old world
*   And shakes us forward and shakes us free*
To run wild with the hope
*   To run wild with the hope*

For most of my working years, I've been employed as a software developer. It was rather comical the first year after college – I had gotten a degree in electronics engineering and then just a few months out of school, I realized that I hated working with circuit-boards and was much more interested in writing software. Talk about four years and $45,000+ down the drain! Thankfully, the Lord opened several doors for me to make the transition into software development within only a few years without having to go back to college to get the proper degree and training. Now I've been working in that field for the last twenty years and am still quite content about how I make a living. And no, I won't fix your computer!

There are moments when I think that in a very miniscule way, I'm contributing to the problem of America becoming more complex and dependent upon technology. I suppose that all of us living in this society contribute to those dependencies in our own tiny ways by just buying electronics and participating in it every day. But there isn't really anything we can do about it, and the truth remains that with or without technology, the world is passing away. The Lord has His plan and He's working it out to completion, and mankind in all our vanity, technology, and cleverness couldn't stop it even if we tried.

The current phase of God's plan for this world is calling out a special people for Himself, people from every nation, tribe, and language (Matthew 24:14, Revelation 5:9). Once He is finished and the last member of the Church has been added, He'll remove the Church from the world and begin working through Israel again as described in Revelation and most of the Old Testament End Time prophecies (Romans 11:25, 1 Thessalonians 4, 2 Thessalonians 2, Revelation 7). Over the last century, He has been regathering the Jewish people to their homeland, which He scattered more than 2,000 years ago but promised to regather in the latter days.

The verse where God "shakes us forward and shakes us free" perfectly describes salvation and what He desires of us: to be shaken free of this world so we can walk with Him. This world has its hooks and barbs in us from even before we're born and they only sink in deeper over time – until we're saved and we begin a relationship with Jesus Christ, the Overcomer and Redeemer of the world. As James 4:4 states, *"Do you not know that friendship with the world is enmity with God? Whoever therefore wants to be a friend of the world makes himself an enemy of God."* Though we're still in this world, we are not to be of it – we have been called out of it (1 Peter 2:9-10, John 17:14-15).

Along with being called to be fellow heirs with Christ (Romans 8:16-17), the concept of being called to liberty is unique to the Bible, as far as spirituality is concerned. Throughout the Bible, liberty is proclaimed, from its earliest stories of Noah, Abraham, Joseph, and of course, the freeing of the Hebrew slaves from Egypt. However, these were only types or models provided for us – the ultimate liberty is the liberty of being set free of this fallen world of sin.

"And you shall know the truth, and the truth shall make you free...Therefore if the Son makes you free, you

shall be free indeed...Stand fast therefore in the liberty by which Christ has made us free, and do not be entangled again with a yoke of bondage. For you, brethren, have been called to liberty; only do not use liberty as an opportunity for the flesh, but through love serve one another. For all the law is fulfilled in one word, even in this: 'You shall love your neighbor as yourself.'" – *John 8:32,36; Galatians 5:1,13-14.*

When Jesus began His ministry in Nazareth, consider the first passage He read (Luke 4:16-30) which is from Isaiah 61: *"The Spirit of the Lord is upon Me, because He has anointed Me to preach the gospel to the poor; He has sent Me to heal the brokenhearted, to proclaim liberty to the captives and recovery of sight to the blind, to set at liberty those who are oppressed; to proclaim the acceptable year of the Lord."* His friends and neighbors enjoyed His sermon so much that they responded by hauling Him out of town and attempting to throw Him off a cliff (Mount Precipice)!

What does it really mean to be free? Is it being able to do whatever we wish whenever we wish it? No, that's licentiousness, which quickly leads to debauchery and then slavery to sin. True freedom is living with purity and integrity and being blameless before our Creator. True liberty is being remade in His likeness and being free of this fallen world of sin, even while we still walk in it. God sent His Son to free us from our shackles of sin and even the law of sin and death by taking our punishment upon Himself on the Cross.

Jesus came to proclaim liberty to the captives of this world and shake us free of it. That's the entire premise of the Bible, the whole story of redemption from when Adam and Eve ate of the fruit and became slaves to sin all the way to the last page of Revelation where God brings the New Jerusalem to earth to dwell with us.

We Christians have been redeemed for the sake of liberty and are called to daily live in liberty, to run free with Him and experience as much of His creation as we possibly can – to run wild with the hope of an eternal future with Him.

7. Elijah

*"My favorite song that I've ever written is 'Elijah.' I
wrote it around the time when John Lennon was shot. He
was a big hero of mine, and my great-grandma died about
the same time. I began thinking about the influence both of
those people had on my life, and they were dead. These two
people would never know the impact they had on me; John
Lennon I'm sure would never care to know, but my
great-grandma, I never got to tell her. But then I realized I
don't have to tell her. She didn't do what she did to have
some kind of an impact on me. She did what she did because
that's who she was. And I'm going to be dead someday too,
and I wanna die good." – Rich Mullins*

The song "Elijah" is about our often-weary life on this
earth and how he would like to go out in a blaze of glory
straight up to Heaven like Elijah. This song was one of the
first of Rich's that really struck a chord within me. Maybe it
was because I have this thin somewhat-fatalistic streak
inside that sometimes pops to the surface, in that I imagine
going out that way too.

After visiting Israel, whenever I hear the song today I
cannot help but remember touring the Stella Maris
Monastery on Mount Carmel, which is dedicated to the
prophet Elijah. What makes it particularly memorable is
their large stone statue of Elijah standing on the neck of a
false prophet with an upraised knife just outside the main
building. The monastery is located several hundred feet

above the place where Elijah slew the 850 false prophets, which looks out over the huge Jezreel Valley. The ancient name for this valley is the Valley of Megiddo – or Armageddon.

While it's not always obvious from the Scriptures, many of the battles in the Old Testament occurred in this same valley. The geography of Megiddo almost forms a gate between the north and the south of Israel, from the coast to the rest of the land. Have you ever considered why Israel is such a special place in God's eyes? Could it be that it's because Israel is at the junction of the three largest continents, and in order to pass between them, the travelers had to go through Israel? In the middle of that juncture is Megiddo, and in ancient times the king who controlled Megiddo could control the trade-routes and traffic between all three continents. And it's in this very place where the King of King will put down all the armies of mankind when He returns.

Elijah was one of two people in the Old Testament who never experienced death, the first being Enoch before the Flood, in which it is written that he walked with God and God took him. The picture of this I like best is where God and Enoch are walking together one day and God says, "We're much closer to My place than yours, so why don't you just come home with Me?" As quaint as that picture may be, I can't imagine Enoch or Elijah (or any of us who want to be with God) declining His invitation!

Elijah
2 Kings 2:11; Matt 6:19-21

The Jordan is waiting for me to cross through
*   My heart is aging I can tell*
So Lord, I'm begging for one last favor from You
*   Here's my heart take it where You will*

*This life has shown me how we're mended and how we're
torn*
How it's okay to be lonely as long as you're free
Sometimes my ground was stony
And sometimes covered up with thorns
And only You could make it what it had to be
And now that it's done

Well if they dressed me like a pauper
Or if they dined me like a prince
If they lay me with my fathers
Or if my ashes scatter on the wind
I don't care

But when I leave I want to go out like Elijah
With a whirlwind to fuel my chariot of fire
And when I look back on the stars
It'll be like a candlelight in Central Park
And it won't break my heart to say goodbye

There's people been friendly,
But they'd never be your friends
Sometimes this has bent me to the ground
Now that this is all ending
I want to hear some music once again
'Cause it's the finest thing that I have ever found

But the Jordan is waiting
Though I ain't never seen the other side
Still they say you can't take in the things you have here
So on the road to salvation
I stick out my thumb and He gives me a ride
And His music is already falling on my ears

There's people been talking

Walks With Rich

They say they're worried about my soul
Well, I'm here to tell you I'll keep rocking
   'Til I'm sure it's my time to roll
And when I do

When I leave I want to go out like Elijah
   With a whirlwind to fuel my chariot of fire
And when I look back on the stars
   It'll be like a candlelight in Central Park
And it won't break my heart to say goodbye

'Cause when I leave I want to go out like Elijah
   With a whirlwind to fuel my chariot of fire
And when I look back on the stars
   It'll be like a candlelight in Central Park
And it won't break my heart to say goodbye

There are two versions of this song – the original which was released on Rich's first album and the remake, which is the one usually played on the radio. Personally, I prefer the original to the remake, mostly because it's much more raw and passionate. You can clearly hear Rich's deep, honest yearning for God to take him home and set him free of this world of sin and heartache.

Coincidentally, Rich died in a tragic car accident. While it's not entirely clear who was driving, since it was Rich's jeep it's likely that he was the driver. Evidently he fell asleep at the wheel and the jeep veered into the other lane of traffic; he overcorrected and was thrown onto the road and then hit by a truck. He was gone in an instant. And while he didn't go to Heaven on a literal chariot of fire, I imagine he was just happy to get there without a lot of pain and suffering.

The Jordan is waiting for me to cross through
   My heart is aging I can tell

So Lord, I'm begging for one last favor from You
Here's my heart take it where You will

The reference to crossing the Jordan River throughout the Scriptures is much more than just passing over a river, it's about entering into the Promised Land, whether it's the literal land of Israel or Heaven. After being to the Jordan River, it's nothing like most of us from the United States would imagine – the Jordan River is roughly 160 miles long and about as wide and deep as some of our creeks, though it does widen and flow faster at flood-stage. Israel is about the size of New Jersey, and it seems like every little hill, valley, or stream has been named at one time or another. It's often tough not to have the same reaction as when seeing Plymouth Rock for the first time: "That's it?!?"

As we go through life in this fallen world, it does indeed age our hearts, especially as we draw closer to God and further away from the world. Rich wrote this song in his early twenties when he had just begun his music-career and before his nearly-constant touring. However, it seems that his heart lightened as he learned to focus more on Jesus rather than the dichotomy between the heavenly world he yearned for and the fallen one he lived in.

The verse "here's my heart, take it where you will" is taken almost verbatim from the chorus of "The Breaks" (or vice-versa), and is the core of our personal struggle with God. In fact, this verse has been particularly hitting home with me over the last year as I've been forced to do some heavy heart and soul searching. The current lesson I'm undergoing is letting the Lord take my heart where He will, because I seem to do a pretty terrible job of it when I chase after my own desires. Psalm 37:4 says, *"Delight yourself also in the Lord, and He shall give you the desires of your heart."*

Isn't that what God wants most from us: our hearts and our devotion – our deepest intimacy? But those cannot be taken, not even by God – true devotion and intimacy can only be given. It's one thing to DO daily devotions by reading the Bible and praying, but quite another to BE devoted daily to Christ. Being devoted to Christ is a series of moment by moment, day by day decisions that are continually made in our hearts and minds and expressed in our attitudes and deeds.

This life has shown me how we're mended and how we're torn
How it's okay to be lonely as long as you're free
Sometimes my ground was stony
And sometimes covered up with thorns
And only You could make it what it had to be
And now that it's done

So much of life is about being torn, mended, and then retorn and remended. That's how muscle is built, and also how our spirits are conformed to His – by being repeatedly broken and then remade, by being pressed and squished and then reshaped. In numerous places in the Bible, God promises to wound but also bind up, to break and then remake: *"For He bruises, but He binds up; He wounds, but His hands make whole...Come, and let us return to the Lord; for He has torn, but He will heal us; He has stricken, but He will bind us up...'Now see that I, even I, am He; and there is no God besides Me; I kill and I make alive; I wound and I heal; nor is there any who can deliver from My hand."* (Job 5:18; Hosea 6:1; Deuteronomy 32:39)

The idea of freedom with loneliness strikes me as relating to painful, failed relationships. Is it really okay to be lonely as long as you're free? Yes and no – I think it depends on what exactly you're free from. If you're in a good relationship, you won't really be free or lonely, though if you're in a bad relationship (such as a dying marriage), you won't be free but can be extremely lonely. A bad relationship – especially a bad marriage – can feel very much like a literal prison at times.

During our engagement, I remember scoffing at the silly notion that sometimes being married can bring intense loneliness and isolation. At the time, that idea made absolutely no sense to me. How could being married possibly lead to loneliness? But our premarital counselor was right – marriage can be very lonely, because loneliness is a matter of relationship rather than proximity. You can be surrounded by hundreds of friendly people and be just as lonely as if you were all by yourself in the middle of the ocean.

A much deeper example of being lonely but free is when we become saved and really start to walk with Christ. Let's face it – when Christ calls you out of the world, He calls you to not only stop going with the flow, but to also go against the world and its desires. Christ calls us to be separate, to be holy, and that means often being alone in this world. But that loneliness is more than worth it, because He has set us free – really, truly free.

Well if they dressed me like a pauper
*   Or if they dined me like a prince*
If they lay me with my fathers
*   Or if my ashes scatter on the wind*
I don't care

In the grand scheme of life, does it really matter where we are buried or how we're dressed? Perhaps to the living, but not to the dead, though the one who died often plans his will and legacy accordingly. In reality, it's like Rabbi Joseph Telushkin's mother once said, "When you're dead, you're dead!" I personally haven't been to very many tombs or mausoleums, but George Washington's grave does stand out to me. As far as American history goes, it's probably one of the most serene places, next to Arlington, Gettysburg, Pearl Harbor, and the other war memorials.

The other graves that come to mind are the Garden Tomb and the Holy Sepulcher in Jerusalem. The difference between the two sites could not be more pronounced. The Garden Tomb is a humble, serene setting in a quiet garden adorned with flowers and simple plaques, while the Holy Sepulcher (the traditional location of Jesus's burial site) is a dark, noisy, crowded, cold granite church littered with jewels, silver, and gold. One is natural, beautiful, and reflective while the other is artificial, cold, and busy. There are numerous reasons why the Garden Tomb is likely the true site for Christ's burial and resurrection, but to me the simple humility and beauty of the place in contrast to the other speaks volumes.

In the end, it really doesn't matter where we're buried – only that we're raised from it – regardless of where that happens to be!

There's people been friendly,
But they'd never be your friends
Sometimes this has bent me to the ground
Now that this is all ending
I want to hear some music once again
'Cause it's the finest thing that I have ever found

This verse is another one that resonates deeply with me. As we go through our days, how often are we surrounded by friendly, polite people, yet we so often have very few genuine friends? I think that it's infinitely better to have one or two deep, close personal friends who will stick with you through thick and thin than a thousand pleasant acquaintances.

When I stop and think about it, music really is a great mystery. Somehow music can touch our souls in profound ways that poetry or mere melodies simply cannot. It's almost as if our hearts were made for music and music was made for our hearts. There will be much music in Heaven, and after hearing our Master's Voice, I imagine that music is what we'll hear after we finally reach our Home.

But the Jordan is waiting
  Though I ain't never seen the other side
Still they say you can't take in the things you have here
  So on the road to salvation
I stick out my thumb and He gives me a ride
  And His music is already falling on my ears

Along with the allegory of "crossing the Jordan" as going to Heaven, I love the picture of us sojourners and vagabonds down here on earth sticking out our thumbs to catch a ride from the King. Here we are, tired, hungry, and exhausted from walking along these dusty roads of earth; we see Him coming and we put out our thumbs hoping He'll see us. He's probably driving an old pickup truck rather than a stretch-limo. We have nothing to offer Him in return for His grace and mercy, and we both know it. Nevertheless, the King pulls up next to us and says "Hop in! I know where you want to go! You're with Me!"

There's people been talking
  They say they're worried about my soul
Well, I'm here to tell you I'll keep rocking
  'Til I'm sure it's my time to roll
And when I do

Few things grate on my nerves as much as gossip and being overly judgmental, particularly within a church. But the funny thing is, I've always been very judgmental too – or at least I was until I went through my divorce. That experience has left me rather humbled and unassuming about people, and that's a good thing. Just as no one can know the true condition of a marriage, family, or friendship except those directly involved, so no one can know the true relationship between a believer and their God. I am certain we will be utterly astonished when our true relationships are revealed someday.

Rich was quite an unconventional, non-traditional type of Christian, and often that rubbed the conservatives and traditionalists the wrong way. Personally, I tend to lean rather conservative and traditional because that's how I was raised (Methodist and Mennonite, then ended up more or less nondenominational). However, I think we all need to be shaken out of our comfort-zones and look deeper than merely the shiny surface for a change. If Jesus were to walk into our churches today, would He be wearing a three-piece suit and $100 tie? I highly doubt it. But He likely wouldn't be wearing ripped jeans and an obnoxious T-shirt either. He would probably just be Himself and would wear whatever was needed to get His message across.

When I leave I want to go out like Elijah
*   With a whirlwind to fuel my chariot of fire*
And when I look back on the stars
*   It'll be like a candlelight in Central Park*
And it won't break my heart to say goodbye

For those of us who walk with Christ and yearn for our Home, when it comes our time to die, will we really look back at this earth much? Will it really break our hearts to leave the world and all its vanities behind? Speaking for myself, I will miss those I may leave behind, but I will not miss this world, particularly with my sights set on my true Home.

If it really breaks our hearts to say goodbye to this world, then maybe we don't yearn for Heaven as much as we should...

8. Growing Young

*"There's a line out of G. K. Chesterton where he says
how we hate monotony because we're not strong enough to
exult in it. He says children kick their legs rhythmically out
of an excess, not a lack of life. How do we know that all
daisies are alike not because they have to be but because
God never gets tired of making them? How do we know the
sun doesn't rise every morning because God says, 'Do it
again'? It might be due to the abundance of God's life that
the universe continues without variance. Then he says, we
have sinned and grown old and our Father is younger than
we."* – Rich Mullins

"Growing Young" is a song about us all being spiritual
prodigal sons and daughters, how the world whispers certain
secrets to us and lures us with delectable sins that only weigh
us down and age us. As our innocence slips away, we
spiritually age and grow old, tired, and worn out. The Gospel
and Christ's work of renewal in us is about restoring that
sweet innocence in our minds and hearts and freeing us from
those heavy burdens of sin that have accumulated over the
years.

Christ came to set us free from sin (Luke 4:16-30) and
give us new life not only for the world to come, but for the
world we're currently in. When we become saved, eternal
life isn't something we're given after we die – we have
eternal life the instant we become part of His family. It's just
that our earthly bodies will die upon death, but that's okay –

He promises to give us new bodies, wonderful bodies made out of stuff that lasts.

Growing Young
Matt 19:13-14; Luke 15:11-24

I've gone so far from my home
*   I've seen the world and I have known*
So many secrets
*   I wish now I did not know*
'Cause they have crept into my heart
*   They have left it cold and dark*
And bleeding,
*   Bleeding and falling apart*

And everybody used to tell me big boys don't cry
*   Well I've been around enough to know that that was the*
lie
That held back the tears in the eyes of a thousand prodigal
sons
*   Well we are children no more, we have sinned and grown*
old
And our Father still waits and He watches down the road
*   To see the crying boys come running back to His arms*
And be growing young
*   Growing young*

I've seen silver turn to dross
*   Seen the very best there ever was*
And I'll tell you, it ain't worth what it costs
*   And I remember my father's house*
What I wouldn't give right now
*   Just to see him and hear him tell me that he loves me so*
much

And everybody used to tell me big boys don't cry
  Well I've been around enough to know that that was the
lie
That held back the tears in the eyes of a thousand prodigal
sons
  Well we are children no more, we have sinned and grown
old
And our Father still waits and He watches down the road
  To see the crying boys come running back to His arms

And when I thought that I was all alone
  It was your voice I heard calling me back home
And I wonder now Lord
  What it was that made me wait so long?
And what kept You waiting for me all that time?
  Was Your love stronger than my foolish pride?
Will You take me back now, take me back and let me be Your
child?

'Cause I've been broken now, I've been saved
  I've learned to cry, and I've learned how to pray
And I'm learning, I'm learning even I can be changed
  And everybody used to tell me big boys don't cry
Well I've been around enough to know that that was the lie
  That held back the tears in the eyes of a thousand
prodigal sons
Well we are children no more, we have sinned and grown
old
  And our Father still waits and He watches down the road
To see the crying boys come running back to His arms
  And be growing young
Growing young
  Growing young

When I was growing up in Ohio, we lived in this old
farm-house at the end of a long gravel driveway about a

quarter-mile from the highway where the school bus would stop. The long walk every morning and afternoon was quite daunting at first, particularly in early elementary school – especially when it was freezing cold, raining, or snowing.

Whenever I hear this song, I imagine myself being dropped off at the end of that lane by that big yellow bus and setting off on that long trek back home. I can see my dad working on the house or in the front yard and seeing me a ways off. He stops whatever he's doing and starts heading towards me with a big smile on his face.

That's the heartwarming picture I have for this song, and that's how I imagine our Heavenly Father running towards us when we finally stop slopping around in the pig-pens of this world, repent of our sins, and turn to Him for salvation. He longs to save us and is waiting for us with open arms, but it's up to us to look up from our slop and repent of how we're living.

In the Parable of the Prodigal Son, what was it that made him finally come to his senses and realize he was really languishing in a pig-pen? Being broken – thoroughly, irreparably broken. Being completely helpless and dependent on someone else for his mere survival. Often I think that until we are really broken in spirit, we can't see our true condition and turn to Him for salvation. I don't think we can really cry out to Him until we realize that we have something terrible to cry about.

I've gone so far from my home
I've seen the world and I have known
So many secrets
I wish now I did not know
'Cause they have crept into my heart
They have left it cold and dark
And bleeding,
Bleeding and falling apart

The world teases us with its so-called deep secrets, tantalizing pleasures, and irresistible delicacies of the senses that we can barely imagine. But all these secrets and delights come with a heavy price, which is paid with our innocence and in the end only leaves us with sorrow and burdens. How many of those secrets do we wish we could unlearn or better yet, never have learned in the first place! How much of our innocence has been lost to things that not only cannot satisfy, but weigh down our hearts and burden our souls? How much of our innocence has been stolen without our even knowing it until much later?

How can our lost innocence be restored, our hearts be unburdened, and our minds be cleansed? By focusing on Christ and the continual renewal of our minds, by setting our sights on things above rather than things here below. It's not about trying harder not to sin and not thinking about things we shouldn't, but keeping our hearts and minds focused on Christ. In our flesh, we can do nothing good, but when we yield to the Spirit, God can work through us (Romans 7, John 6:63). The more we wallow in our sins and this worldly pig-pen, the more they cling to us and weigh us down, for with the loss of innocence comes the loss of liberty.

And everybody used to tell me big boys don't cry
   Well I've been around enough to know that that was the lie
That held back the tears in the eyes of a thousand prodigal sons
   Well we are children no more, we have sinned and grown old
And our Father still waits and He watches down the road
   To see the crying boys come running back to His arms
And be growing young
   Growing young

The world can often be a very cold, dark place, and when emotions and feelings are held inside for an extended period of time, the heart begins to grow cold, unfeeling/numb, and eventually bitter. Restoration with God and others can only come once the heart has been softened – or usually broken – and the tears are allowed to flow.

Tears are funny things – they can be shed in times of both sorrow and pain, but also joy and happiness. Often they can express what words simply cannot, what the heart is feeling but cannot be uttered. During the storms of our lives, sometimes when the tears begin flowing, they cannot be stopped no matter how hard we may try. One passage that became very precious to me was Psalm 126:5-6: *"Those who sow in tears shall reap in joy. He who continually goes forth weeping, bearing seed for sowing, shall doubtless come again with rejoicing, bringing his sheaves with him."* That's such a wonderful promise from the Lord, that all our tears are not shed in vain, that they ultimately have a greater purpose: to bring forth a harvest of joy in our hearts!

Several places in the Bible speak of our hearts being like different types of soil, soft and fertile, thorny, or hard and crusted over. In Hosea 4:12, Israel is admonished to *"Sow for yourselves righteousness; reap in mercy; break up your fallow ground, for it is time to seek the Lord, till He comes and rains righteousness on you."* In the New Testament when Jesus gives the Parable of the Sower (Matthew 13), He uses the same metaphors to describe our hearts:

> *"Therefore hear the parable of the sower: when anyone hears the word of the kingdom and does not understand it, then the wicked one comes and snatches away what was sown in his heart. This is he who received seed by the wayside. But he who received the seed on stony places, this is he who hears the word and immediately receives it with joy; yet he has no root in himself, but endures only for a while. For when*

tribulation or persecution arises because of the word,
immediately he stumbles. Now he who received seed
among the thorns is he who hears the word, and the cares
of this world and the deceitfulness of riches choke the
word, and he becomes unfruitful. But he who received
seed on the good ground is he who hears the word and
understands it, who indeed bears fruit and produces:
some a hundredfold, some sixty, some thirty."

One of the jobs we had to do every spring was rototilling
– breaking up the winter-hardened soil before we could plant
the seeds. The soil had to be softened, watered, and fertilized
before it could be of any real use for growing things. The
same holds true with our hearts – if we are not consistently
cultivating a relationship with God and remaining soft, over
time they harden and the weeds of bitterness and numbness
settle in and start to take root. If we are not able (or not
willing) to break up the fallow soil of our hearts, then God
has to if we are to be of any real use to Him. Our hearts need
to be soft and fertile in order for Him to sow His seed and
then grow His crops of grace, compassion, forgiveness, and
mercy.

With years of being hardened and wallowing in sin comes
aging and growing old. You can see it in the countenance,
the posture, and even the health of those who engage in
sinful lifestyles for an extended period of time. Alcoholism,
drug abuse, sexual sins, and other forms of hard living all
eventually take their toll on their abusers, but the first signs
are shown in their dulled eyes and forced smiles. When sin
settles in, the light and brightness of their eyes goes out and
the smiles fade.

As I've recently crossed the threshold into my forties,
I've become aware of new physical changes, especially
since I've been getting back into shape. Most days I still feel
like I'm 22, though I'm quickly approaching twice that age. I
certainly have noticed the changes, such as hair-loss,

needing more sleep, and that it's not as easy to get rid of extra weight (and keep it off) as it used to be. When I hit forty, I began being drawn to things that have more lasting value, such as classical music, an appreciation for art and antiques, playing musical instruments again, and wanting experiences more than stuff. I've always had something of an old soul, and it wasn't too hard to transition into that more mature mindset. Many people struggle with growing older, but I think much of it is all about the attitude rather than simply the years. With the breaking out of my comfort-zone and trying new things, I've noticed that my attitude has changed, and though the years are creeping by, I'm starting to feel younger than I used to and have a sense of newness and purpose.

The Father yearns to restore us and set us free of our sins if we would only repent and seek His face. He yearns to release us from our heavy burdens if we would only just humble ourselves enough to give them to Him! One of the saddest moments in all the Bible is when Jesus was weeping over Jerusalem and He cries that He yearned to gather them under His wings – but they would not (Luke 13:34-35). How many people spurn His incredible invitation to their own eternal demise!

He yearns to restore our innocence and help us grow young and free again – but the question is: "Will we let Him?" Jesus has practically given us a free ticket into Heaven and an invitation to eternal life, but it's up to us to accept that invitation and redeem that golden ticket! He can't accept it for us, but He's done everything else. He cannot compel us to be with Him regardless of how much He wants to. Love is a choice, a decision – and He wants us to choose Him of our own free will.

I've seen silver turn to dross
Seen the very best there ever was
And I'll tell you, it ain't worth what it costs

And I remember my father's house
What I wouldn't give right now
　Just to see him and hear him tell me that he loves me so
much

My first real job after college was at Silicon Graphics (SGI), one of the top companies in the technology capital of the country (yes, there were other tech companies before Google and Facebook). In the mid-1990s, SGI's claim to fame was that they had helped make "Jurassic Park" and started the boom in CGI back in the day (their computers were even featured in the movie). One of the first things I noticed about the Silicon Valley culture was that work was life, that so many there live to work instead of work to live. Growing their careers and climbing the ladder are practically their idols, and many don't even realize it until it's too late.

I worked at two different start-up companies in a very short period of time, and I worked with some of the Valley's best and saw how empty and pointless it was in the end. How many of those rising Silicon Valley stars are now burned out has-beens? How many have sacrificed their youth, friends, families, and marriages on the altar of technology and careers? I personally know several, and I'm certain there are tens of thousands more just like them.

One of the most precious things for any person of any age is to hear their father say they love them. Of course, they like hearing Mom tell them that too, but everybody knows that! But there's something special about hearing a father express their love, because it usually doesn't come easy for them. I have been blessed with a great father who still looks out for us and frequently expresses his affection through phone calls and handwritten letters (unfortunately, I have atrocious handwriting and usually reply with email). As a father myself, I do my best to show affection to my own children and let them know they will always have a safe place they can call "home" with me, wherever I may happen to be.

So many of America's problems – along with so many of the world's problems – begin in the home with fathers not being engaged, committed, loving, or even sticking around very long. As my own marriage has broken apart, we have done as much as we can to keep our home stable despite the deterioration of our marriage. How I wish more fathers would remain engaged and involved with their children, even if they cannot stay with their mother! Sometimes simply being there is all that's needed, but we fathers are called to much, much more.

It's been said that most people tend to form their perception of God according to their personal relationship with their own fathers. If their earthly fathers are absent, uncommitted, abusive, or quick-tempered and angry, then that's how they'll tend to see their Heavenly Father. But if their earthly fathers are patient, loving, committed, and forgiving, then that's how they'll tend to view God. More than anything else (apart from salvation), the world needs good fathers, fathers who love their children and regularly show it, men who love their wives, and who are committed, sacrificial, and live with integrity.

And when I thought that I was all alone
*   It was your voice I heard calling me back home*
And I wonder now Lord
*   What it was that made me wait so long?*
And what kept You waiting for me all that time?
*   Was Your love stronger than my foolish pride?*
Will You take me back now, take me back and let me be Your
child?

Several characteristics of great fathers are their unwavering patience, commitment, persistence, and their rock-solid love. Great dads remain steady through their kids' prodigal-years and do their best not to take their stinging insults and moments of immaturity and downright rebellion personally. A great dad will continue to love them and wait for their kids to come back around to them, to patiently wait for them until they realize they really don't have all the answers (usually in their 20s or 30s or even 40s!) and that their parents really did want what was best for them, even if they didn't agree about much of anything else.

Great mothers and fathers love until it hurts and wounds them, but even then they keep on loving their kids. They forgive all the insults, barbs, bad attitudes, and acts of rebellion. Sooner or later, love wins – just like with us and our Heavenly Father.

'Cause I've been broken now, I've been saved
I've learned to cry, and I've learned how to pray
And I'm learning, I'm learning even I can be changed

Our sinful hearts are like young, stubborn horses – they must be broken to be of any use to our Master. To make matters worse, many of us are like wild mustangs that need to be repeatedly broken over an extended period of time for those lessons to finally stick. Because of our pride, hard hearts, and stubborn, pig-headed will, we need to be broken for the Father to finally get through to us and to finally be useable to Him.

In my own personal life, I have been broken several times – so far. The first was soon after I left home and finally hit "the wall" and came to the end of myself. God used that breaking to finally reach me and bring me to Himself. The second time was over my impure thought-life and not guarding my eyes and thoughts like I should have, and I was taken to the proverbial woodshed. The most recent time has been over the past year or two as my marriage has collapsed. For much of our marriage, I could not cry nor could I pray as I should have. But once I was broken, the tears and prayers began to flow (usually together!) and haven't really stopped.

I'd like to offer some personal advice about sin for a few moments. First, and foremost, guard your heart and keep focused on the Lord and growing closer towards Him. Proverbs 4:23 says, *"Keep your heart with all diligence, for out of it spring the issues of life."* For this verse, I personally like the World English Bible translation better, which reads *"Keep your heart with all diligence, for out of it is the wellspring of life."* A big part of guarding your heart is taking your thoughts captive (2 Corinthians 10:5) and confessing your sins early, often, and honestly (1 John 1:9). If you don't guard your heart and take those sinful thoughts captive, before long they harden your heart and start to steal your soul.

Next, cowboy (or cowgirl) up and take your lumps and chastisements sooner rather than later! You cannot hide or bury your sin no matter how hard you may try. As Galatians 6:7-8 states, *"Do not be deceived, God is not mocked; for whatever a man sows, that he will also reap. For he who sows to his flesh will of the flesh reap corruption, but he who sows to the Spirit will of the Spirit reap everlasting life."* Most assuredly, God will never, ever ignore or shrug at your sin, and you will have to deal with the consequences sooner or later – and the longer you wait, the worse they become and the harder your heart grows! Sowing and reaping is a spiritual law and cannot be skirted – period. All sin comes with a price, so just accept that terrible truth, confess your sins, and get the punishment over with as soon as you can before it hardens your heart – or worse!

If you're caught in a tangled web of sin, lies, and cover-ups, don't think for an instant that God cannot forgive them, not matter how bad they may be. In fact, He already forgave all your sins at the Cross and He offers you restitution and reconciliation, but you have to accept it. Though the consequences and chastisement for your sin might be tough, God offers you His grace and a new life free of whatever sin you're dealing with. Psalm 119:67 says,

"Before I was afflicted I went astray, but now I keep Your word." With loving correction and a tender heart comes obedience, and not just out of fear of additional chastisements, but out of love and wanting to please God more than delighting in your sin. While I was growing up, I had more than my share of spankings, and through them I learned the difference between right and wrong, as well as the value of obedience because I knew how much my father loved me. And please know that our Heavenly Father loves us much, much more than our earthly fathers ever can!

Though I had long ago made a covenant with my eyes (Job 31:1-4), before I was afflicted, I went astray. The problem with my own sin and most others began in my mind with an impure thought-life and then began infecting my heart. I stopped taking those little thoughts captive and let down my guard, and then let my eyes and mind venture off to wherever my flesh wanted to go. Like when David committed his sin with Bathsheba, it wasn't in a challenging time that I wandered away, but when everything was going pretty well. It's when the stock-market is up and profits are at an all-time high when the biggest crashes happen. The first rumblings of a fall are felt when we are self-confident, secure, and complacent.

How do you battle your flesh day after day over a long period of time? By consistently starving it and putting those sinful desires to death as described in Romans 8:1-8. Remember, we're in a spiritual WAR with our flesh and its desires, not a friendly little game of ping-pong:

> *"There is therefore now no condemnation to those who are in Christ Jesus, who do not walk according to the flesh, but according to the Spirit. For the law of the Spirit of life in Christ Jesus has made me free from the law of sin and death. For what the law could not do in that it was weak through the flesh, God did by sending His own Son in the likeness of sinful flesh, on account of sin: He*

condemned sin in the flesh, that the righteous requirement of the law might be fulfilled in us who do not walk according to the flesh but according to the Spirit. For those who live according to the flesh set their minds on the things of the flesh, but those who live according to the Spirit, the things of the Spirit. For to be carnally minded is death, but to be spiritually minded is life and peace. Because the carnal mind is enmity against God; for it is not subject to the law of God, nor indeed can be. So then, those who are in the flesh cannot please God."

Resisting your flesh is a moment by moment battle (particularly at first), and especially if you're addicted to whatever sin you're caught up in. Sins are very much like weeds – the longer you let them go, the deeper their roots will grow and the more they will enslave your heart and destroy your life. No matter how much you try to ignore them and pretend that they're really not that bad, the harder you're making it on yourself when the time finally comes to pull them. You have a choice: either you can pull those weeds or eventually God will pull them for you. Remember, He loves you too much to allow you remain in your sin and let it destroy you. All sin comes with consequences that will have to be dealt with sooner or later – sowing and reaping is a spiritual law that cannot be skirted. Take those little thoughts captive and pull those weeds early before they become monsters that turn you into their slave!

Do whatever you need to starve your flesh and win the battle, and I do mean WHATEVER it takes. Don't be afraid to be ridiculously extreme when you're being tempted – remember that the goal is to defeat your flesh. First, pray for the strength and grace to resist it, then take action against it: unplug the TV, lock up the computer, hide your phone, take a long drive, or go running in the middle of the night – do whatever it takes to flee from temptation! Personally, I get on the treadmill for a while with my Kindle or do pull-ups and push-ups (sometimes a LOT of push-ups). The temptation you thought would never end usually only lasts a few minutes, but integrity, purity, and blamelessness last much, much longer!

1 Corinthians 10:13 promises both faithfulness from God and His deliverance in those tough moments: *"No temptation has overtaken you except such as is common to man; but God is faithful, who will not allow you to be tempted beyond what you are able, but with the temptation will also make the way of escape, that you may be able to bear it."* But even though He may give you that escape (and He will!), you still have to choose to take it, to turn towards God and away from your flesh. You are always given a choice – the only question is whether you will choose to obey God or obey your carnal desires (your flesh).

After you have some victories against your particular sin under your belt, you'll start to realize that the next temptation can be resisted too, and then the next one after that. As you start to rack up victories and time goes by, the idea of blowing your winning streak begins to help you resist those temptations too. The good news is that those battles will gradually get easier (usually), but the bad news is that if you think you can go back and dabble or indulge a little in your own personal sin, you'll most likely fall and have to fight those first battles all over again, and next time they might be much harder! If you really want to live to please God, you'll stop indulging your flesh and surrendering to your sin, because willfully sinning while trying to please God is completely incompatible (and impossible!).

There's an old proverb that says "Clean living is its own reward." While that may certainly be true, clean living, regularly confessing your sins, and living with personal integrity and purity is critical to maintaining a close, intimate relationship with the Lord. You cannot boldly approach His throne of grace while hiding your sin or sweeping it under the rug (believe me, I've tried!). There is nothing better than being able to pray with a clear conscience and speaking with Him as you would with a friend in which there are no secrets between the two of you. 1 John 3:3 tells us that if we are saved and wish to grow closer with God, we will purify ourselves.

Being broken is very tough and nothing short of heart-wrenching at times, and so many of us just want it to be over with as quickly as possible so we can get on with our normal lives. However, there is a certain sweetness in being helpless and broken. The intimacy I have experienced with God over the last few years has been nothing like I've ever known. The Bible (particularly the Psalms) have meant more to me than ever before, and God has felt closer than I could've ever thought possible. Though I frequently desire this time of brokenness and remaking to end, at the same time I don't.

Above all, I do not want to lose this newfound intimacy and dependence on God. I do not want to lose my integrity and purity and clear conscience with God. If the Lord can bring me through the death of my marriage and the subsequent divorce with my integrity and purity intact, then He can bring me through anything – including all those sinister little complacent times when everything is going great. I want to be guiltless when I kneel before Him every day. I want to be blameless so I can boldly approach His throne of grace. I want to be daily growing closer to Him and becoming more like Him. And if that means that I must dwell in this spiritual olive-press for a very long time, then so be it.

Above all, we must seek true intimacy with our Creator, Savior, and Lord Jesus Christ.

9. Hard to Get

"There are many things in the Christian faith that are hard to get a handle on, and one of the things that I struggle the hardest with is believing that God really loves me. It's too good to believe, but it's true. Whether I can believe it or not. The fact is, I think if you took the whole Bible and you shook it around and melted it down and said, 'what is the essence of what this whole thing is saying,' I think it would just be that God loves you very much. That God in fact is crazy about you." – Rich Mullins

Of all the songs on "The Jesus Record/Demos," this one is probably my most favorite, and though it's rather rough, I prefer Rich's raw version to the produced one. Both the song and the catchphrase "Hard to Get" has a double-meaning, that Jesus can often be very hard to take hold of and also be very hard to understand. God has this wonderful way of being simple enough for a child to understand and follow, while at the same time utterly confounding and mysterious to even the most enlightened theologians.

Seeking out the depths of God and His heart is like trying to find the bottom of a crystal-clear tropical sea. Just when you think you've almost reached it, you find that it's still deeper and more mind-blowingly beautiful than you could have ever imagined.

If one didn't know better, God makes Himself tough to understand on purpose, so that we keep seeking after Him, poking at Him, and experiencing Him to know more about

Him. To grow in deeper and deeper intimacy with Him. To know that He is more real than the earth under our feet and the air inside our chest.

"Hard to Get" is about a broken man crying out to Jesus and asking if He knows how tough it is down here and if He remembers what it was like walking through this heart-breaking, painful world. Does He remember what it was like to lose someone He dearly loved? Does He remember what it was like to be abandoned and betrayed by those He loved? Does He remember feeling everything we feel?

I contend that not only He does remember, but that He knows those feelings at a depth we cannot even fathom.

Hard to Get
Psalm 77:7-13; Isa 53:4; Isa 55:8-9; Matt 5:4; Matt 6:11; Luke 22:41-45; Rom 7:18-19,24-25

You who live in heaven
  Hear the prayers of those of us who live on earth
Who are afraid of being left by those we love
  And who get hardened by the hurt

Do you remember when You lived down here where we all scrape
  To find the faith to ask for daily bread
Did You forget about us after You had flown away
  Well I memorized every word You said
Still I'm so scared, I'm holding my breath
  While You're up there just playing hard to get

You who live in radiance
  Hear the prayers of those of us who live in skin
We have a love that's not as patient as Yours was
  Still we do love now and then

Did You ever know loneliness
   Did You ever know need
Do You remember just how long a night can get?
   When You were barely holding on
And Your friends fall asleep
   And don't see the blood that's running in Your sweat
Will those who mourn be left uncomforted
   While You're up there just playing hard to get?

And I know you bore our sorrows
   And I know you feel our pain
And I know it would not hurt any less
   Even if it could be explained

And I know that I am only lashing out
   At the One who loves me most
And after I figured this, somehow
   All I really need to know

Is if You who live in eternity
   Hear the prayers of those of us who live in time
We can't see what's ahead
   And we cannot get free of what we've left behind
I'm reeling from these voices that keep screaming in my ears
   All the words of shame and doubt, blame and regret

I can't see how You're leading me unless You've led me here
   To where I'm lost enough to let myself be led
And so You've been here all along I guess
   It's just Your ways and You are just plain hard to get

When you stop and think about it, God really is hard to
understand sometimes – even to those who know Him well.
If God is so good, then why is this world bad so much of the

time? If God is really so loving, then why is there so much pain and suffering all around us? If God is so good, then why does He allow our loved ones to be stolen from us? If God is so compassionate, then why does He allow so much suffering in this world? It's very easy to let these doubts and questions overtake us and tear down what meager faith we may have.

That's where holding fast to God and striving to know more of Him (or knowing Him more intimately) with each passing day steps in. An infinite God isn't necessarily supposed to be understood by the finite mind of man. That's one of the many reasons why He had to take the form of a man in Jesus Christ, so we could really relate to Him and so that we could know assuredly that He can relate to us. The only true mediator between God and man must be the God-man, either the man who became God or the God who became a man – and since the first option is impossible, the second was the only solution to bridging the gap between us. The Creator Himself put off His glory and became a man so as to pay the penalty for our sins and redeem us unto Himself.

Why does God do things that seem strange or even downright weird to us sometimes? For His glory and His purposes, to show us that despite our profound wisdom, His "foolishness" is infinitely wiser still. As Paul writes in 1 Corinthians 1: 20-25:

> *"Where is the wise? Where is the scribe? Where is the disputer of this age? Has not God made foolish the wisdom of this world? For since, in the wisdom of God, the world through wisdom did not know God, it pleased God through the foolishness of the message preached to save those who believe. For Jews request a sign, and Greeks seek after wisdom; but we preach Christ crucified, to the Jews a stumbling block and to the Greeks foolishness, but to those who are called, both Jews and*

Greeks, Christ the power of God and the wisdom of God.
Because the foolishness of God is wiser than men, and the
weakness of God is stronger than men."

On a more practical level, why would we even want to
follow any god who doesn't know what it's like to live down
here? Why should we follow after Allah, Ba'al, or Zeus who
hasn't experienced this life as a human being? How can they
relate to how we feel and how we suffer if they haven't felt
or suffered as we do? Maybe that's why so many people are
fascinated by those who purport to become enlightened, that
they may think they've reached that next step towards
godhood, that they can become gods themselves (Genesis
3:5).

That's why Jesus is infinitely different than every other
supposed God-man or man-made god: Jesus has dwelt
among us and has tasted death and despair like we will. He
does know what it's like to walk a mile in our shoes (and
then some!). What a comfort it is to know that He has felt
everything that we feel and that He has been tempted in
every way that we have! What a comfort it is to know that
He not only sees and hears us, but that He KNOWS us and
what we're doing through!

Do you remember when You lived down here where we all
scrape
    To find the faith to ask for daily bread
Did You forget about us after You had flown away
    Well I memorized every word You said
Still I'm so scared, I'm holding my breath
    While You're up there just playing hard to get

The idea that Rich expresses of us "scraping for the faith
to ask for daily bread" is such a vivid description of our
struggles at times. Sometimes we open our Bibles and see
only words. Sometimes we get down on our knees, bow our

heads, and then nothing comes out. Sometimes we just groan for the Lord when the pain is so sharp or deep that it's simply inexpressible.

Faith doesn't come easy for most people at times, and suffering tends to reveal the true quantity and quality of faith we really have. Let's face it: it's tough to hold onto your faith when you're broken and struggling, particularly over an extended period of time. It's tough to keep your head up when you're unemployed or sick or heart-broken. It's hard to keep the faith when you're in a difficult marriage or in an angry, abusive home. It's difficult to believe that better, brighter days are ahead when all you see before you is darkness and hopelessness.

Those dark times are when we tend to cry out to God the most, but even then it often feels like He's just not there, that He's playing "hard to get" for some reason. But those are only our feelings and perceptions, not reality. And that's where drawing upon the truths from the Bible and our prior experiences of God's faithfulness are so important when we're struggling, so that we will KNOW that He is with us in our struggles even when we can't feel His Presence. Passages like Psalm 34, Psalm 73, and the Beatitudes of Matthew 5 are tremendous comforts when we are suffering and broken. To know that God is with us even when we're convinced that He isn't – He might just be carrying us in His arms like the one in the "Footprints in the Sand" poem.

Almost immediately after being broken and coming to Christ years ago, there were several instances where I know for certain that God intervened to provide for me. Twice I went completely broke and was about two weeks from having to move back home with my tail between my legs, and He provided jobs or money right out of the blue to help me remain in school. He has blessed me with reliable transportation at the times I needed it the most, and the same with layoffs and new job opportunities at the various companies I've worked at. Over and over in my life, God has proven Himself to be faithful and true, even when I wasn't.

Did You ever know loneliness
  Did You ever know need
Do You remember just how long a night can get?
  When You were barely holding on
And Your friends fall asleep
  And don't see the blood that's running in Your sweat
Will those who mourn be left uncomforted
  While You're up there just playing hard to get?

Loneliness was something that Rich struggled with for a large portion of his life, regardless of how popular he was and how well his albums were selling. Loneliness isn't simply about being alone, it's about feeling alone, and sometimes loneliness is at its worst when you're surrounded by people. How many mothers are painfully lonely though they're surrounded by a brood of children they dearly love? How many people are desperately lonely though they're married, even when they're in an arguably decent marriage? How many kids are lonely on the playground or in the classroom though they're surrounded by friends?

Loneliness is a dark specter that can creep over you even when you're not alone, wishing to pull you away from faith and hope. Loneliness can be often felt when you can't sleep, when your mind starts spinning out of control and playing tricks on you. Yet it is those same dark watches of the night when God can also be the closest and most present. As He says in Deuteronomy 31:6, *"Be strong and of good courage, do not fear nor be afraid of them; for the Lord your God, He is the One who goes with you. He will not leave you nor forsake you."* God is with us whether it's when we're about to go off to battle or when we're lying awake in the middle of the night.

Jesus knew intense loneliness, and I would venture to guess that He was lonely most of the time. I expect that He was often frowned upon and whispered about, being the supposed illegitimate son of Mary. If that wasn't bad enough, I'd imagine that just Him being sinless would tend to isolate Him from many potential friends and even His family at times. After all, He wouldn't exactly have been up for sneaking off to go fishing with His brothers when Joseph and Mary were trusting Him to be doing the chores.

Even during His ministry when He was surrounded by the adoring crowds and His inner circle of the Twelve, He was lonely. Though they had followed Him through thick-and-thin for three years and seen all sorts of miracles and wonders, when He needed them the most – when He needed them to be faithful for a mere hour or two – they let Him down. Jesus was probably at the loneliest, darkest point in His life in the Garden of Gethsemane, and the disciples' napping likely made it much worse.

And I know that I am only lashing out
  At the One who loves me most
And after I figured this, somehow
  All I really need to know

This verse has always hit home with me, and I'm often stopped in my tracks when my own children lash out at me in a fit of anger. Particularly when kids are little, they get upset without really knowing why, and then they lash out at their parents (often their mother), who loves them the most. How thoughtless and cruel it is when we do that to our own children or our spouses or even to God, to those who love us the most?

There were moments when my marriage was falling apart (and afterwards) that I was sometimes unexplainable angry, frustrated, and grieved. There were times when I asked God why He hadn't intervened in our relationship and why He wasn't doing anything to stop what was happening. There were times when I just didn't understand much of anything, and it was all I could do to keep going through my day. But at night, the questions and doubts would arise, and the temptation to accuse God of wrongdoing would swell. As a parent, I know full-well that when the words "It's not fair!" pop out of my heart (and mouth!), I'm throwing a temper tantrum instead of praying.

Thankfully, most of us usually come to our senses after our little temper tantrum is over and apologize, though it may be a long time afterwards.

Is if You who live in eternity
*   Hear the prayers of those of us who live in time*
We can't see what's ahead
*   And we cannot get free of what we've left behind*
I'm reeling from these voices that keep screaming in my ears
*   All the words of shame and doubt, blame and regret*

For much of my life, I've had this mental painting of what my future would be like and where I was headed. A lifetime of hopes and dreams naturally paints a beautiful picture. Though I couldn't see their faces or know their names, I always felt relatively certain that someday I would be married and have a couple of children along the way. Over time as those dreams were realized and the details filled in, that painting has become clearer, along with other events starting to take shape in the background, such as a career, the teenage years, emptying the nest, weddings and grandkids, and eventually retirement and the "golden years."

But then the unexpected happened – the death of my marriage and the subsequent divorce – and now that painting has been ripped off the wall and thrown in the trash. It cannot be repaired, much less restored. Suddenly, I find myself rather directionless for the first time in two decades and standing at a crossroads with a thousand different paths available, yet with absolutely no idea which one to set off on.

Gradually a new mental painting will take shape, but at this point there are only dim shapes in the background, shapes such as writing, working, traveling, and volunteering. Perhaps this time it would be better to let God paint that picture for me instead of me pushing Him off to the side (or even behind me!) and scribbling with the brushes how I think it should look. Maybe this time I should just let the Master Painter of Life do His thing and I stand back and watch His handiwork for a change.

The central verse "We can't see what's ahead and we cannot get free of what we've left behind" is particularly painful at times, as the future I saw for so long has now been torn away. Yet even though that painting has been discarded, I still cannot completely break free of what has been lost. I will always remember that beloved painting that I gazed upon and labored over for half my life, though it will never be a reality. Not even the great Gabriel Allon of Daniel Silva fame could restore that painting – but God can if He so chooses.

And those voices – those relentless tormentors named Shame, Doubt, Blame, and Regret – how they always seem to know just the right words to twist the knife to make it go deeper still! We all hear them at different times in our lives, some of us more loudly and more often than others. What can make those voices become fainter or even fall silent? The voices of Forgiveness, Grace, Hope, and Love – those voices that come from God and His Word rather than the ones which come from our Accuser and our own Self.

I can't see how You're leading me unless You've led me here
To where I'm lost enough to let myself be led
And so You've been here all along I guess
It's just Your ways and You are just plain hard to get

One of the more humbling (and frightening) experiences is to be blindfolded and led somewhere you're completely unfamiliar with. It's not nearly as bad if you trust whoever is leading you, but being at the complete mercy of someone else can be very debilitating. In the self-defense class I've been taking, we're often forced to close our eyes before being attacked so we can get used to being caught completely off-guard, to rely upon our training to react according to what we've been taught rather than just our instincts. Being in a debilitating situation forces you to rely upon something greater than what you can simply see, hear, and feel all around you.

The funny thing is though, that that's often where God places us in order for Him to be able to finally work in our hearts and to learn to fully rely upon Him: He allows us to come to a frightening place of complete dependence and blindness so we have no option other than to trust Him and His Word. It's easy for most children to trust because they know little cruelty and evil (hopefully), but for us who are older and have been hurt, trust can be very difficult and challenging, if not impossible. The old phrase, "Let go and let God!" may sound quaint, but often that's what He really wants from us. How does one learn to trust again, and even have some of that innocent, childlike trust? Through love, faith, and time – trust requires all three to be healed and rebuilt.

A big part of trust is allowing ourselves to be led. Often when I walk our two Labrador retrievers, they'll catch the scent of a rabbit or raccoon and pull incessantly towards it until either I give in and let them go or I pull them back onto the path and they forget about it. But I never let them go, because they could get hurt or bitten. It's so much easier to walk them when they simply let me lead them and keep them on the narrow path where they're free from thorns, burrs, and wild animals.

How often the same is true with God and us! How often do we strain at His gentle leash on our lives, yearning to chase after whatever we desire for that fleeting moment, regardless of how much trouble we might bring upon ourselves! Sometimes He releases us for a while so we can get into trouble and hopefully learn from our mistakes, though many of us are thick-headed and require multiple lessons. But even when He releases us to our headstrong ways, He is still there and will draw close to us when we cry out to Him.

How much easier it is to simply let Him lead us on His narrow path through this life rather than our ever-changing, wandering ways!

Walks With Rich

10. Heaven in His Eyes

"Some of us are so afraid that God's not going to look at us. So we're out there doing all sorts of things to get God to take notice, but folks, God notices you. The fact is, He can't take His eyes off of you. However badly you think of yourself, God is crazy about you. God is in love with you. Some of us even fear that someday we'll do something so bad that He won't notice you anymore. Well, let me tell you, God loves us completely. And He knew us at our worst before He ever began to love us at all. And in the love of God, there are no degrees, there is only love." – Rich Mullins

This is one of those handful of songs written at the very beginning of Rich's musical career but not released/published until more than twenty years later. For me, "Heaven in His Eyes" always conjures up vivid memories of Israel, particularly around the Sea of Galilee and in the nearby cities where Jesus preached, taught, and lived.

The Sea of Galilee (or Kenneret) is really more of a big lake fed from the Jordan River that originates from Mount Hermon in the north. The Sea is roughly 13 miles long by 8 miles wide and is Israel's primary freshwater source. In Israel, it's known as the Sea of Life, while the Salt Sea (the Dead Sea) is the Sea of Death. Galilee was one of Jesus's favorite places to live, with the Jewish cities mostly along the western side, while along the east is the Decapolis,

Gadara, and the place where the possessed pigs drowned (the place of the "devilled ham").

During His earthly ministry, Jesus spent most of His time in and around Capernaum, one of the larger ancient cities along the northern side that is literally a few feet from the Sea. The ruins of Peter's house are there, along with a partially-restored synagogue where Jesus attended and taught on a regular basis. The Israel Antiquities Authority has done an excellent job in reconstructing the city, and beautiful flowers frequently line the paths and gardens.

Heaven In His Eyes
Matt 14:22-33; Mark 4:1; Mark 11:27-33; Luke 8:49-55

See the Teacher sitting on a mountain
See Him walking along the shore
Friends and disciples gathering around Him
Say never spake a man like this before

But why's a man as wise as He
Weeping alone in Gethsemane
Did He know some would never see
The heaven in His eyes

See the Master walking on the water
Hear Him speak and calm an angry wave
Look at Him raising up Jairus's daughter
And with a word Lazarus comes forth from the grave

But why is a man as strong as this
Being betrayed by a good friend's kiss
Could it be that maybe this man missed
The heaven in His eyes

I'm not talking about the pie in the sky

That you good boys and girls get in the by and by
But rather the strength, the strength that we can find
  If we've got the guts to try

See the Teacher playing with the children
  Hear Him baffle doctors of the law
Look at the people gathering to go with Him
  Those who see the vision that He saw

This is why a man as holy as He
  Had to die alone on Calvary
It was the only way that we could ever see
  The heaven in His eyes

The heaven in His eyes
  The heaven in His eyes
Yeah, the heaven in His eyes
  The heaven in His eyes

Have you ever considered what made Jesus so different than everyone else when He was on earth? Sure there were the miracles He performed and such, but those often only drew crowds for a very short time. What made the disciples drop everything they were doing – their entire lives, families, friends, and businesses – and not only follow Him, but stick with Him for the next three years? It was the "Heaven in His eyes."

I believe that it was the reality of another world that shown in His face, gleamed in His eyes, and echoed through His voice. It's that reality of a whole other world that's all around us, that spiritual world of something much greater and fantastic that we can possibly even imagine. Heaven isn't something or someplace that we can see, hear, smell, and feel with our earthly senses, but we all somehow know it's there. Yet it's impossible to get there even though it's so close we can almost taste it at times – well, it's impossible to get there without Jesus.

When Jesus came to earth, His Home began to shine through and touch everyone around Him. Some drew close to that Light for a time and then pulled back, others didn't want to see it at all and stayed in the darkness, while others found that Light to be utterly irresistible and clung to it with everything they had. It's that Light that makes some of us toss everything else aside and chase after Him with everything we have.

How many of us see the light He offers when we open our Bible? How many of us want to stay in darkness and close the Book as fast as we can? How many of us follow Him for a short time but then return to our comfortable, dimly-lit lives? And how many of us can't resist that Light and want to experience more of Him with everything that's within us?

Jesus is that Light – the Light of the world.

11. Hold Me Jesus

"This [Hold Me Jesus] is a song I wrote in Amsterdam, and kind of how everything is 'legal' in Amsterdam. I always thought my parents didn't sin because they were just too old. When I was there, I was as old as my parents were when I used to think that. And I don't think I was – I guess you just think that as you live, you eventually outgrow temptation, and the reality is, you don't. You need Jesus just as much now as you ever did." – Rich Mullins

Along with "Elijah," this is another one of Rich's songs that has always hit close to home with me, particularly the bridge that begins with "Surrender don't come natural to me..." Rich's quote above sums up something I have felt for a long time but was never quite able to articulate. For as far back as I can remember, I figured that someday I would be wise enough to be free of my own personal stumbling-blocks, weaknesses, and faults and then live out the rest of my days in relative ease and comfort.

However, as I've grown older (and somewhat wiser, I hope) the reality is that though we may conquer our stumbling-blocks and shore up the defenses in our weak areas, there are still many more battles to fight. As long as we walk this earth, there will never be a time when we lapse into relative ease. What about the so-called golden-years that so many of us long for after our careers wind down? Those supposed carefree, sunny days are often fraught with loss of energy, memory, and health. Every year in this world brings a new set of challenges and problems, and so it will be until we are finally called Home.

The best we can do in this life is to accept our lot and cling to the Lord, and this song "Hold Me Jesus" sums up that reality perfectly.

Hold Me Jesus
1 Kings 19:3-13; Matt 11:25-30

Well, sometimes my life just don't make sense at all
 When the mountains look so big
And my faith just seems so small

So hold me Jesus, 'cause I'm shaking like a leaf
 You have been King of my glory
Won't You be my Prince of Peace

And I wake up in the night and feel the dark
 It's so hot inside my soul
I swear there must be blisters on my heart

So hold me Jesus, 'cause I'm shaking like a leaf
 You have been King of my glory
Won't You be my Prince of Peace

Surrender don't come natural to me
 I'd rather fight You for something I don't really want
Than to take what You give that I need
 And I've beat my head against so many walls
Now I'm falling down, I'm falling on my knees

And this Salvation Army band is playing this hymn
 And Your grace rings out so deep
It makes my resistance seem so thin

Walks With Rich

I'm singing hold me Jesus, 'cause I'm shaking like a leaf
  You have been King of my glory
Won't You be my Prince of Peace

You have been King of my glory
  Won't You be my Prince of Peace

If we're brutally, painfully honest with ourselves, we humans really are a pathetic bunch, even though we often can't admit it (or simply won't). Spiritually speaking, we wander all over the place and can barely keep focused for a fifteen-minute sermon these days. Though we often think otherwise, we have very little control over the most basic things in our lives such as food, water, clothing, and shelter. One little accident, snowstorm, tornado, or earthquake and everything we always take for granted is thrown out the window and our true dependence and fragility is revealed.

So what's the best we can really do in this crazy, messed-up world we find ourselves in? Hang on and cling to the Lord with all that we have, because when we're honest, that's all we can really do. A word closely related to dependence is brokenness, because one frequently reveals the other. When all your wheels fly off your car or the cheese keeps falling off your cracker or you just can't quite make that last piece of life's puzzle fit, that's about being dependent and broken.

Brokenness feels horrible, yet it's during those times of utter dependence that our true condition is revealed to us. When we're having a relatively normal day and the sun is shining and the birds are chirping, God often gets pushed to the back-burner. Our true, desperate need for Him is easily clouded, and our dependence upon Him is frequently marred by our own meager accomplishments. And then the clouds roll in, the lighting strikes, and the thunder booms, and we suddenly discover that we're not so big and strong after all.

We suddenly find ourselves cowering under the covers praying desperately for the storm to end!

So often we want to resist God, particularly when He is working on breaking us down and softening our hard hearts (Hosea 10:12). The soil of Colorado is filled with bentonite, a type of clay that expands unevenly in moisture, which is a big problem for the foundations of homes and other buildings. When it's hot and dry (which is about all the time), it can become about as hard as concrete, and water just runs right off of it. In the fall we have droughts and the spring we have flash-floods. Forget roto-tilling that Colorado soil to break it up – you need a pick-ax and a sometimes even a jack-hammer!

Sometimes that's what must be done with our sundried, hardened hearts – the fallow ground needs to be smashed and broken up even before it can be softened. No one likes to be broken, but sometimes there's just no other way for Him to get through to us. Sometimes the Potter has to crush the shoddy clay ashtray we've slapped together before He can begin shaping and molding His masterpiece.

Surrender don't come natural to me
I'd rather fight You for something I don't really want
Than to take what You give that I need
And I've beat my head against so many walls
Now I'm falling down, I'm falling on my knees

Surrender can be many different things, but it's never easy, and it certainly isn't enjoyable or natural! Surrender is often humiliating, hopeless, and crippling, and our natural, inborn pride rebels against the very notion of surrender with everything we have. "Never surrender!" is engrained into our very Self at the deepest levels!

Several of the books in the Old Testament are about surrender, particularly the book of Jeremiah. A significant portion of his ministry was convincing his own people to surrender to the Babylonians, to simply stop resisting and submit to Nebuchadnezzar's rule. But they would not, and by refusing to obey, they lost their temple, city, and sovereignty and were exiled from their homeland for seventy years.

Though God had raised up the Assyrians and the Babylonians to punish His stubborn, disobedient children, He didn't want to destroy them – they did that all by themselves by refusing to surrender as He had repeatedly beseeched them to do. They destroyed themselves by refusing to submit to His will, namely surrendering to the Babylonians. Since the book of Jeremiah isn't chronological in places and sometimes difficult to understand, Thom Lemmons wrote an excellent fictionalized version of the book called "He Who Wept," which made the entire book practically come to life! The book of Jeremiah is all about seeing God in the midst of brokenness and learning to trust Him even everything's literally going to "Hell in a Hand-basket" and when all is lost.

As hard as it may be to admit, the same disease of pride and hard-heartedness that destroyed ancient Israel is often found inside all of us. How often do we destroy our own lives by refusing to submit to God's pleadings for us to surrender? How often do we rush full-steam ahead chasing after something we think we want rather than listen to God's gentle whispers of "Not yet" or "Be patient"? How often do we beat our heads against these brick walls until we lose consciousness, only to wake up and then do it all over again?

How utterly human it is for us to "fight God for something we don't really want, than to take what He gives that we need?" If that doesn't sum up our fallen, tragic condition, then I don't know what does. What does God want from us down here? In this battle of wills and hearts, what will make the war end? Nothing short of unconditional surrender from us – surrender of our pride, our will, our heart, our mind, and our very Self.

But with that humiliating surrender of Self comes peace, restoration, and wholeness – and an entirely new life in Christ. Look closely at what Ezekiel 26:26 and 2 Corinthians 5:17 say – *"I will give you a new heart and put a new spirit within you; I will take the heart of stone out of your flesh and give you a heart of flesh...Therefore, if anyone is in Christ, he is a new creation; old things have passed away; behold, all things have become new."* When Christ saves people, He doesn't just fix or improve our hearts, He gives us an entirely new heart and a new life in Him. Only through this new heart of surrendering to Christ can we finally be victorious in this world, even if our outward circumstances may not improve (or even worsen!). Only through surrender to His will can we finally become the people we were created to be.

What exactly is it that He gives that we need (and often so desperately need)? God gives us lots of things, but the greatest thing He can ever give us is His Love! He offers it freely and repeatedly, and how often do we spurn Him or ignore His gentle overtures to us? How often do we open every other door except His that has been open to us the entire time?

Jesus said in Matthew 22:37-40 that the greatest commandment was to love the Lord your God with all your heart, all your soul, and all your mind, and that the second greatest commandment was to love your neighbor as yourself. I can understand there being a commandment to love our neighbors, but why is there a commandment to love God? Also, why is THE greatest commandment to love God? It's not a suggestion or even a wise piece of advice, but a real commandment just like "'Don't steal', 'Don't murder', and 'Don't commit adultery!'"

I think we're commanded to love God because sometimes – especially when tragedy strikes and that to which we hold most dear is torn away from us – it's not very easy to love God. It's not easy to love God when our parents grow old and pass away. It's not easy to love God when we are betrayed by someone we love, someone who we thought loved us. It's not easy to love God when one of our children suffers or even dies. It's not easy to see evil and wickedness and injustice all around us and wondering why God doesn't do something about it.

But loving God is what we must do regardless of what befalls us – there is really no other option in this life. He is the Keeper of Life and Death, Hope and Love, Joy and Sorrow, and He has promised us that all things work together for good, for those who love Him. He has a plan for those who love Him, to make us like His Son, to change us from slaves dead to sin to living heirs of His Kingdom (Romans 8:28-30).

Walks With Rich

12. Home

"Friends, don't be afraid to go home. The Heavenly Father is waiting. Not because He wants to give you a whipping. Not because He wants to rub your nose in your failures, but because He had a Son who was a composite failure. He had a Son who tried to have this great ministry, had thousands of followers. His Son chose for Himself, He had twelve people on His staff. In three years' time He had managed to alienate every person in one way or another. He died His Father's Son, stricken with grief, so overloaded with guilt that He had to look away, His Father could not look at Him." – *Rich Mullins*

"Home" is a beautiful song that portrays our resurrection, those first incredible moments after we breathe our last breath and our hearts beat their last beat. Those first moments of the rest of our eternity. Those first glimpses of the real world in which we can finally see, hear, smell, touch, and experience the Creation as it was always meant to be. The first glimpses of our new Home. I always imagine our Savior watching our eyes flutter open, flashing a huge grin at us, and then whispering, "You can breathe now!"

This fallen world was never meant to be our final destination – we're just passing through as a fleeting vapor, a mist in the wind. Hebrews 13:14 declares *"For this world is not our home; we are looking forward to our city in heaven, which is yet to come."* Someday, that day shall come and we will truly be home! Someday, the words of 1 John

3:2 will be fulfilled in each of us personally: *"Beloved, now we are children of God; and it has not yet been revealed what we shall be, but we know that when He is revealed, we shall be like Him, for we shall see Him as He is."*

Someday, we shall see Him as He is – and also see everything and everyone else as they really are too!

Home
Isa 60:1-3; 1 Cor 2:9; 2 Cor 4:7-18; 2Tim 2:11-13

I see the morning moving over the hills
*   I can see the shadows on the western side*
And all those illusions that I had
*   They just vanish in Your light*
Though the chill in the night still hangs in the air
*   I can feel the warmth of morning on my face*
Though the storm had tossed me
*   'Til I thought I'd nearly lost my way*

And now the night is fading and the storm is past
*   And everything that could be shaken was shaken*
And all that remains is all I ever really had

What I'd have settled for
*   You've blown so far away*
What You brought me to
*   I thought I could not reach*
And I came so close to giving up
*   But You never did give up on me*
I see the morning moving over the hills
*   I feel the rush of life here where the darkness broke*
And I am in You and You're in me
*   Here where the winds of Heaven blow*

And now the night is fading

And the storm is through
And everything You sent to shake me
  From my dreams they come to wake me
In the love I find in You
  And now the morning comes
And everything that really matters
  Become the wings You send to gather me
To my home
  To my home
I'm going home

"Home" is a wonderful word, and an even more wonderful concept. Home brings up thoughts and feelings of family, comfort, welcome, safety, familiarity, laughter, and rest. Some of my fondest memories of home are of being with family, playing games, and reading books on lazy afternoons or quiet evenings.

There have been at least a dozen different places I've lived, but only two I have really thought of as "home." The first was my childhood home out in the country halfway between Bryan (home of the Etch-a-Sketch and Dum-Dums) and West Unity, a small town where I went to school. The second has been my home just north of Denver, though we had moved here to be close to my ex-wife's family. Since my divorce, I must say that Colorado hasn't really felt much like home since most of my family is on the other side of the Mississippi. So I suppose I'll be looking for another place I can call my home one of these days, probably somewhere much, much closer to a beach!

Not to be too morbid, but "Home" is the first of two songs of Rich's that I have always imagined being played at my memorial service. Whenever I listen to this song, I can almost see the first rays of that morning sun breaking on the eastern horizon, burning through all that lingering fog and driving away the long, cold night. A big smile breaks out on my face at the warmth and brightness of that pure light and then I open my eyes to finally behold Him in all His glory.

With the breaking of the dawn comes a new day and with it, a whole new life on a whole new, better world. A perfect world. A world free of sin, pain, and death. As 1 Corinthians 13 says, *"For we know in part and we prophesy in part. But when that which is perfect has come, then that which is in part will be done away... For now we see in a mirror, dimly, but then face to face. Now I know in part, but then I shall know just as I also am known."* All those things that couldn't be discerned during that long night have now been made clear, and we can live freely without fear.

I see the morning moving over the hills
   I can see the shadows on the western side
And all those illusions that I had
   They just vanish in Your light
Though the chill in the night still hangs in the air
   I can feel the warmth of morning on my face
Though the storm had tossed me
   'Til I thought I'd nearly lost my way

And now the night is fading and the storm is past
   And everything that could be shaken was shaken
And all that remains is all I ever really had

When the brilliant rays of that first new day of Eternity strike us, our old lives will rapidly fade away with the fleeing night. All those dark times, those terrible storms, and those crushing trials and struggles we never thought would end will be over and vanish behind us as we face that new everlasting morning. And though down here we all too often question whether our faith is really worth all the trouble, in that instant we will know for certain that it most assuredly was. Every moment of heartache, every lonely night, every day of struggling to just get out of bed only to do it all over again will have been worth it. More than worth it!

The verse "And all that remains is all I ever really had" is one of those poetic verses that helps put things into the proper perspective – the eternal perspective. Since we know from 2 Peter 3:10 and Revelation 21 that one day God is going to toss this current universe in the trashcan and create an entirely new one, what do we really have that will last? All that will remain of us is how we loved God and loved one another, and how we glorified God with our lives. 1 Corinthians 3:11-15 says that:

> *"For no other foundation can anyone lay than that which is laid, which is Jesus Christ. Now if anyone builds on this foundation with gold, silver, precious stones, wood, hay, straw, each one's work will become clear; for the Day will declare it, because it will be revealed by fire; and the fire will test each one's work, of what sort it is. If anyone's work which he has built on it endures, he will receive a reward. If anyone's work is burned, he will suffer loss; but he himself will be saved, yet so as through fire."*

Without a doubt, our seemingly-endless struggles in this fleeting life will be incomparable to the ravishing glory and the boundless eternity that awaits us (Romans 8:18).

One of my favorite books in the Bible is the book of Job, with the key verse for me being Job 1:21b (especially over the last year): *"The Lord gave, and the Lord has taken away; blessed be the name of the Lord."* I don't know what else I could have done to save my marriage, but it died nevertheless, and God is to be praised regardless of whether I am married or divorced, healthy or sick, rich or poor, happy or sad. Job exemplified this deep personal commitment to God by not sinning or charging Him with wrongdoing during his terrible trials (which probably lasted several months or more), and God listed him as one of the three greatest men in the Old Testament in Ezekiel 14:14 alongside Noah and Daniel.

I first became interested in Job when I heard it was the oldest book of the Bible and had all sorts of curious treasures in it, especially in the last several chapters when God speaks about His creation and how He carefully watches over it. In fact, I like the book so much that the last novel I wrote before my marriage fell apart was a fictionalized version of the book of Job called "Out of the Whirlwind." I've thought about changing the dedication since it was to my former wife, but I meant what I wrote at the time. I hate it when others rewrite history, so I figure I shouldn't either.

The other key passage for me in the book is Job 19:25-27, which is one of the greatest verses about the Resurrection in the Bible. Considering that the passage is at least 4,000 years old, it indicates that the ancients long before Abraham knew that a divine Mediator was needed to bridge the chasm between God and mankind, and that one day He would physically reign on the earth and that the believers would be physically resurrected:

> *"For I know that my Redeemer lives, and He shall stand at last on the earth; and after my skin is destroyed, this I know, that in my flesh I shall see God, whom I shall see for myself, and my eyes shall behold, and not another. How my heart yearns within me!"*

The first time I really connected with this passage was right before I had an informal interview over dinner with a couple of executives at a startup company in Santa Clara. I knew both were cool towards Christians (with one being downright antagonistic), and I was skimming the Bible for some courage and reassurance for the evening, regardless of whether I got the job or not. Anyway, this verse jumped off the page at me and gave me one of those "cling-to" passages

I've cherished ever since. Notice that Job doesn't say *"I think my Redeemer lives"* – he says *"I KNOW my Redeemer lives"* and that's something incredibly reassuring to me. Not that it's really related, but I ended up getting that job which put me on the career path I've been on since 1999 (software development).

What I'd have settled for
  You've blown so far away
What You brought me to
  I thought I could not reach
And I came so close to giving up
  But You never did give up on me
I see the morning moving over the hills
  I feel the rush of life here where the darkness broke
And I am in You and You're in me
  Here where the winds of Heaven blow

How often are we tempted to settle for "good enough" in this life, never realizing that God has intended so much more for us? How often are we tempted by those intense, delectable sins without ever bothering to count their true costs in the light of the rest of our lives, much less the light of Eternity? Is that fleeting moment of sin worth a lifetime of heartache? Is that fifteen minutes of adultery or pornography worth the destruction of your marriage and family? Is your sin worth a lifetime of broken trust and shipwrecked faith that will likely propagate to your children and grandchildren? Is that hour of compromise worth your very soul? May it never be!

Consider the life of David for a moment – from the Bible, David is remembered primarily for two things, one of which he is no doubt deeply ashamed of. David is known best for his courage in slaying Goliath, but also for his adulterous relationship with Bathsheba, which resulted in the murder of her husband and the sword never leaving David's house. Not only did that sinful decision haunt him the rest of his life, it dramatically affected all the generations that came after him. Then to really top things off, David's sin has been written into the very Word of God and has been exposed to millions upon millions of people – and will be for all eternity!

So many times in this life we are tempted to just stop striving and fighting our sin and just lay down, to give up and let this world carry us where it may. But though we are tempted to give up, God is not – He will never give up on us and will continue to be faithful even when we have fallen badly and proven to be rather faithless. Though we may stumble and be shaken to our very core, He is not – He cannot. He will remain true and faithful to us regardless of how far we may stray. He knows the End from the Beginning and that first moment in which we gaze upon Him is at His fore-thoughts continually, like parents eagerly anticipating the first sight of their newborn baby.

And now the night is fading
  And the storm is through
And everything You sent to shake me
  From my dreams they come to wake me
In the love I find in You
  And now the morning comes
And everything that really matters
  Become the wings You send to gather me
To my home
  To my home
I'm going home

The crescendo at the end of this song is the part that always gets to me, probably as Rich always intended it to. As I grow older and gradually fade away, I hope that I'll have the attitude of one who is entering the home-stretch, that with every aging, joint-popping step I take, I'm that much closer to my real home. Rather than looking back at this old life that is ebbing away, I want to look ahead to the completion of my race with joy and anticipation, setting aside every weight and sin that hinders (Romans 12:1-2).

When my crumpled, worn-out body has breathed its last and I awaken to Eternity, I want my first thought to be "Hallelujah! I'm finally Home!"

Walks With Rich

13. Jacob and Two Women

"Once you become a teenager, the scariest thing in life, in all of life, is the whole thing of being in love. I think it's a very – you put yourself in a very precarious place when you decide to do that. I have this theory about marriage and singleness. My theory is that – well, my dad gave me this really great advice one time. He said, 'If you can live without her, do.'" – Rich Mullins

"Jacob and Two Women" is a memorable song about the middle years of Jacob's life after he flees from his brother Esau all the way up to Haran, where he falls in love with the beautiful Rachel and lands on the receiving end of a real schemer, his father-in-law Laban.

I've always liked this song but it doesn't really have many profound meanings for me other than some of Rich's infamous prose in the last few verses. The main message of the song is that life is often messy and usually doesn't turn out the way we expected it to, much less how we dreamed it would. In fact, the history of the world is one of fallenness, messiness, and unexpected tragedies. But through it all, God has His plan and He's working it through to completion, no matter how badly we screw things up down here.

What was the greatest spiritual moment in Jacob's life? It wasn't when he saw the angels descending on the heavenly ladder, and it certainly wasn't when he tricked his brother (and father) out of his birthright or when he high-tailed it out of Haran with his father-in-law's flocks. One of Jacob's noblest moments was when he agreed to work as a shepherd seven years to marry Rachel and then even after being deceived on his wedding night, he loved her so much that he worked seven more years for her. If that isn't love, I don't know what is!

In my opinion, the greatest moment in Jacob's entire life was when he was wrestling with the angel, likely the pre-incarnate Christ. Even after he was debilitated with his hip out of joint, he still clung to God with everything he had and wouldn't let Him go.

That is the perfect picture of faith that each of us needs to have: hanging onto our Lord with everything we've got, and even when we're crippled and crushed, still not letting go of Him. But fear not – He holds us in the palm of His hand and won't let us go either (John 10:28).

Jacob and Two Women
Gen 29:16-30

Jacob, he loved Rachel and Rachel, she loved him
And Leah was just there for dramatic effect
Well it's right there in the Bible, so it must not be a sin
But it sure does seem like an awful dirty trick
And her sky is just a petal pressed in a book of a memory
Of the time he thought he loved her and they kissed
And her friends say, "Ah, he's a devil"
But she says, "No, he is a dream"
This is the world as best as I can remember it

Now Jacob got two women and a whole house full of kids
And he schemed his way back to the Promised Land
And he finds it's one thing to win 'em
And it's another to keep 'em content
When he knows that he is only just one man

*And his sky's an empty bottle and when he's drunk the ocean
dry*
   Well he sails off three sheets to some reckless wind
And his friends say, "Ain't it awful"
   And he says, "No, I think it's fine"
And this is the world as best as I can remember it

Now Rachel's weeping for the children
   That she thought she could not bear
And she bears a sorrow that she cannot hide
   And she wishes she was with them
But she just looks and they're not there
   Seems that love comes for just a moment
And then it passes on by

And her sky is just a bandit
   Swinging at the end of a hangman's noose
'Cause he stole the moon and must be made to pay for it
   And her friends say, "My, that's tragic"
She says, "Especially for the moon"
   And this is the world as best as I can remember it
And this is the world as best as I can remember it

Close your eyes and imagine Jacob's home-life for a
minute. Here he had to live with two back-biting, quarrelling
sisters and he's married to both of them and has two of their
maids as his concubines! Either there were no laws for
divorce in Haran or staying married to Leah was part of the
agreement he had worked out with his conniving
father-in-law Laban. Either way, his home was not a happy
one, as evidenced by how most of his sons turned out. They
were known for tossing their own brother Joseph in a cistern
and then selling him into slavery, as well as slaughtering an
entire city after tricking the men into circumcising
themselves.

The most-forgotten person in Jacob's story is Leah, his first wife. Imagine walking in her shoes for a while, being rejected, alone, and unloved while your husband is in the next room with your younger, prettier sister night after night. To make matters worse, since Leah's married and unable to divorce, she's unable to find a love of her own without being accused of committing adultery. And it's not just for a few months or years in that state, but for her entire life!

God could have made Leah beautiful and attract a man on her own, but He didn't for some reason. He knew how much pain she would experience by being rejected and unloved by her husband, but He allowed it anyway. Why? The answer is at the end of the story. Something tells me that Leah grew on Jacob over time, especially after Rachel died. Jacob may have been initially drawn to Rachel by her outward beauty, but he may have been drawn to Leah later by her devotion, service, and faithfulness.

In their family story in Genesis, Leah proved to be the better wife and mother than Rachel by honoring and relying upon God, not clinging to her father's idols, and remaining faithful to her husband even though she was unloved. It's interesting to note the meaning of the names of Leah's children in Genesis 29 and how her focus changed from seeking to attract her husband to praising God. Though she was rejected by her husband, she became a woman of faith and was later esteemed by him. In the end, Jacob honored Leah by having her buried next to his father and mother, where he was also later buried. In the end, Leah proved to be the woman of faith, not Rachel.

I love what Rich said in the quote for "All the Way My Savior Leads Me" in that wherever you find yourself in life, God calls you to be faithful. If you are married, God calls you to be faithful in your marriage. If you are single or divorced, God calls you to be faithful in your singleness. The real kicker about faithfulness is that there are no exceptions or asterisks to it – you're either faithful or you're not, and like love, faithfulness is a choice. We are called to be faithful regardless of what storms are raging all around us and regardless of how unhappy we may be in our present circumstances.

Walks With Rich

14. Land of My Sojourn

"The hardest part of being a Christian is surrendering and that is where the real struggle happens. Once we have overcome our own desire to be elevated, our own desire to be recognized, our own desire to be independent and all those things that we value very much because we are Americans and we are part of this American culture. Once we have overcome that struggle then God can use us as a part of His body to accomplish what the body of Christ was left here to accomplish." – Rich Mullins

A companion song to "Land of My Sojourn" is "Here in America," which was written before personal computers, cell phones, the Internet, and globalization really began changing the face of the country. Both songs were written to capture the fading glimpses of what America used to be before they vanished into only memories. Tragically, my children will never experience the United States I grew up in, that decent country I knew and loved.

To me, this song is about loosening our grasp on this land that we love and hold so dear and knowing that we're just passing through, that though America has been lovingly referred to as "God's Country" for much of its history, it really isn't. Like every other place in this fallen world, America is merely the land of our sojourn.

Land of My Sojourn

Josh 2:1-24; Psalm 137:1-6; 1 Pet 1:17

And the coal trucks come a-runnin'
With their bellies full of coal
And their big wheels a-hummin'
Down this road that lies open like the soul of a woman
Who hid the spies who were lookin'
For the land of the milk and the honey

And this road she is a woman
She was made from a rib
Cut from the sides of these mountains
Oh these great sleeping Adams
Who are lonely even here in paradise
Lonely for somebody to kiss them
And I'll sing my song, and I'll sing my song
In the land of my sojourn

And the lady in the harbor
She still holds her torch out
To those huddled masses who are
Yearning for a freedom that still eludes them
The immigrant's children see their brightest dreams
shattered

Here on the New Jersey shoreline in the
Greed and the glitter of those high-tech casinos
But some mendicants wander off into a cathedral
And they stoop in the silence
And there their prayers are still whispered
And I'll sing their song, and I'll sing their song
In the land of my sojourn

Nobody tells you when you get born here
How much you'll come to love it
And how you'll never belong here

So I call you my country
And I'll be lonely for my home
And I wish that I could take you there with me

And down the brown brick spine of some dirty blind alley
All those drain pipes are drippin' out the last Sons of
Thunder
While off in the distance the smoke stacks
Were belching back this city's best answer

And the countryside was pocked
With all of those mail pouch posters
Thrown up on the rotting sideboards of
These rundown stables like the one that Christ was born
in
When the old world started dying
And the new world started coming on
And I'll sing His song, and I'll sing His song
In the land of my sojourn

In the land of my sojourn
And I will sing His song
In the land of my sojourn

Over the course of my life, I've had the opportunity to live in and visit just about every region in the country. The place I felt the least at home in was in Silicon Valley, which ironically is where I met my former wife. The lifestyles, values, and the entire spirit of the area ran counter to much of the rest of the country I had experienced. In Silicon Valley, just about everything is overpriced, over-paced, and ever-changing. Literally everything feels like it's running at a break-neck pace, while the destination is always changing every other second. As America has become more technology-driven, the values of Silicon Valley are steadily being adopted by the rest of the country.

Spiritually-speaking, America is very much like ancient Israel – even from her founding, America's story runs almost parallel to Israel's. Both countries were formed and settled by a nation of poor, downtrodden people that were miraculously liberated. Both were given the laws of God and richly blessed as they followed in His ways. Both were founded upon creeds of faith and commandments. Both greatly prospered and spread their influence far and wide – and then both faltered and decayed the further they wandered away from God.

Also like Israel, America just isn't America without God. America was founded to be a land of liberty, a Judeo-Christian nation to shine the light of Christ and liberty across the earth. America was never intended to be a land of unbridled licentiousness and crass materialism – that was already present in England, France, and much of Europe, which our forefathers purposely left behind. Lady Liberty looks more like Kim Kardashian these days than anything else. Yes, our forefathers wanted to prosper, but that wasn't their primary purpose in settling this great land – they came here to freely worship their God and live according to the dictates of their conscience, not the dictates of a king. They came to live in liberty.

Here on the New Jersey shoreline in the
   Greed and the glitter of those high-tech casinos
But some mendicants wander off into a cathedral
   And they stoop in the silence
And there their prayers are still whispered
   And I'll sing their song, and I'll sing their song
In the land of my sojourn

America has always had something of a split-personality; one side is filled with unbridled capitalism and materialism while the other is filled with a desire for righteousness, fairness, and equality. Binding both together in this land is a

127

deep love of liberty and individualism, but both sides have always been rather opposed to one another.

This split-personality is expressed in this song, namely between the glitzy casinos that dot the Jersey Shore and the worshippers slipping away from all the hubbub to pray quietly in a church. I think there's something special about escaping a noisy, crazy place and going to find a place to quietly worship instead of reveling in the party-scene, particularly when you know that you'll probably be the only one there.

One of the books that launched me into historical fiction (and later into writing) was "North and South" by John Jakes. When I lived in Atlanta, I took a weekend trip over to Charleston and walked the Historic Tour and toured several of the streets and buildings described in the book. At one point I stopped in St. Michael's Episcopal Church and was fascinated by the architecture, along with the several hundred years of history – George Washington had even worshipped there in 1791! Then when I visited Boston a few years ago, I toured the North Church where the infamous lanterns were hung, and also the Old South Church. It's amazing to think of how many generations have worshipped in these famous buildings, sang the same old hymns, and prayed to the same Savior that we do!

Nobody tells you when you get born here
How much you'll come to love it
And how you'll never belong here
So I call you my country
And I'll be lonely for my home
And I wish that I could take you there with me

Like tens of millions of others in our country, I deeply love America. I was born and raised in the Corn Belt/Rust Belt where we still said the Pledge of Allegiance every morning before school started. Where I grew up, most people still went to church of some sort every Sunday and divorce and teen-pregnancy were still frowned upon and relatively rare.

But over the last twenty to thirty years, the country I've known and loved has gone through a lot of changes, and mostly not for the better. And the older I've grown – not to mention the closer I've grown to God – the more distant I feel from my country. The last decade or two has made me know for certain that America's problems are not political in nature, but deeply spiritual – and spiritual problems never have political solutions. When America did happen to be blessed with a great political leader, it was only because millions were praying for them to be raised up first. But is America praying today? Most days I don't really think so.

Over the last decade, I have come to identify more closely with Israel than America, particularly with our recent politicians who feel more comfortable with terrorist organizations (like Hamas and the PLO) and less with nations that genuinely want freedom, democracy, and security for their people. But of course, even Israel and similar nations aren't perfect – and can never be without Christ's reign – anymore than America was ever perfect.

While I was in Israel the first time in 2010, I was immediately struck by the stark differences in vibrancy, energy, patriotism, and sense of purpose between Israel and America. For example, everywhere we went throughout the land, we saw Israeli flags proudly being displayed. Sometimes they were large banners draped from buildings and balconies, while other times they were simply stickers on the sides of homes and businesses. But they were there – and they were everywhere.

When I returned to the States, I began looking for our flag everywhere I went – but most of the time I couldn't find it without really trying. In Israel, I could literally stand in any location, look around for a few seconds, and spot an Israeli flag. In the United States, I had to hunt around to find our flag, which is usually confined to government buildings, handfuls of businesses, and private homes. The differences between the outward displays of patriotism between our two nations were quite stark – and they were real.

But it wasn't just the patriotism that was different between our two countries, but the attitudes and our zest for life. In Israel, they seem to be much more motivated to live life today rather than put it off for some other time in the future. If they feel like going to the beach or sight-seeing, they go that day instead of waiting for it. Life isn't taken for granted nearly as much – I suppose that's what happens when you know you could get called up for active military service tomorrow or a missile could hit your house without warning.

Since 9/11, it's felt like America has collectively lost its marbles and any notion of common sense! We seem to have traded our liberty for more security, and in so doing have lost a big part of what it means to be Americans. We take far too much for granted and seem to have no real sense of what really matters anymore, like building our families and communities and passing on our values to the next generation. In Israel, people truly love their land and their country, and there's a vital energy and a zeal for life. They don't entirely trust their government nor rely on those services like too many of us do, and they don't take the government so seriously. They don't live in fear of the TSA, DHS, ATF, FBI, or CPS, or much of their own government because they have all served. The Israelis fear real enemies, those who have sworn to destroy them and take over their land – and that shapes many of their attitudes about living.

And the countryside was pocked
*   With all of those Mail Pouch posters*
Thrown up on the rotting sideboards of
*   These rundown stables like the one that Christ was born*
in

When the old world started dying
And the new world started coming on
And I'll sing His song, and I'll sing His song
In the land of my sojourn

I can particularly relate to this verse because of where I grew up in the Midwest. Just down the road from our country house was this old, faded black barn with a huge Mail Pouch Tobacco poster painted across it. The advertisement had to be at least fifty years old and the barn was more than twice that. I would pass it every day at least twice while riding in the school-bus, and I bet it's still standing today.

The place where I grew up is still there of course, and being a small town in the northwest Ohio, it doesn't feel like it's changed all that much, or at least it's changed rather slowly in comparison to many other places in the country. And of course, that has its pro's and con's. The best things about small towns is that it feels like they never change and that everyone knows everything about everyone else – which also happen to be the worst things about small towns.

In the land of my sojourn
And I will sing His song
In the land of my sojourn

Wherever we happen to find ourselves in this great big world, whether it's in small-town America or a sprawling steel and concrete metropolis on the coast or a remote village on the other side of the world, we Christians should remember that this world is only the land of our sojourn. We are to keep a light touch on this world, because this place really isn't our home – and it never will be. It was never intended to be.

And just as importantly, wherever we happen to find ourselves down here, we're to keep singing Christ's songs

131

and shining that Light that He has placed within us – His Light!

Walks With Rich

15. The Love of God

"If you've ever known the love of God, you know it's nothing but reckless and it's nothing but raging. Sometimes it hurts to be loved, and if it doesn't hurt it's probably not love, may be infatuation. I think a lot of American people are infatuated with God, but we don't really love Him, and they don't really let Him love them. Being loved by God is one of the most painful things in the world, it's also the only thing that can bring us salvation and it's like everything else that is really wonderful, there's a little bit of pain in it, little bit of hurt." – Rich Mullins

"The Love of God" is one of Rich's songs that no matter how many times I listen to it, I still get choked up. If I had to pick another song to be played at my memorial someday, this would be it. When I stop and consider just a glimpse of God's unfathomable love towards us that cost Him so much, I can barely hold myself back from trying to wrap my arms around Him.

I once heard an interesting thought-exercise about God, likely from Chuck Missler or someone he was paraphrasing. If you stop and think about it, God demonstrated His infinite power by creating this incredible, mind-blowing universe out of nothing but His mere words. God demonstrated His infinite creativity, artistry, and engineering-prowess by the limitless variety and intricacies of His Creation. God demonstrated His infinite size and greatness by creating vast, unreachable expanses of space and trillions of stars we have yet to even catch a glimpse of.

But how would God demonstrate infinite justice? What about infinite righteousness? And most of all, what about infinite mercy, forgiveness, and love? Those are the questions that can only be answered at the Cross and at the empty Tomb. How do we know that God really is Who He says He is and that He is the One True God? Because our God sacrificially gave Himself up for us so that we might live with Him for all eternity. No other supposed god, enlightened man, or god-man even comes close.

The Love of God
Rom 8:18-39; Eph 3:14-21

There's a wideness in God's mercy
I cannot find in my own
And He keeps His fire burning
To melt this heart of stone
Keeps me aching with a yearning
Keeps me glad to have been caught
In the reckless raging fury
That they call the love of God

Now I've seen no band of angels
But I've heard the soldiers' songs
Love hangs over them like a banner
Love within them leads them on
To the battle on the journey
And it's never gonna stop
Ever widening their mercies
And the fury of His love

Oh the love of God
And oh, the love of God

The love of God

Joy and sorrow are this ocean
  And in their every ebb and flow
Now the Lord a door has opened
  That all Hell could never close
Here I'm tested and made worthy
  Tossed about but lifted up
In the reckless raging fury
  That they call the love of God

The idea of God having a reckless, raging fury of love for us is from one of Brennan Manning's books, "The Ragamuffin Gospel", from which Rich also borrowed the name of his band, the Ragamuffins. Brennan Manning's simple, concise proclamation of the Gospel made such an impact in Rich's life that it marked a turning point for him, which was expressed in his music – and particularly with this song. Rich told the story of his first encounter with Manning as follows:

> *"... Beaker put in a Brennan Manning tape and I really didn't want to hear it because I didn't know who he was and don't ordinarily like preaching. I went "Argh, great." Well, I think about five minutes into it, I think I had to pull off the road because I was just bawling my eyes out. I thought, what I am experiencing here is that I have gone to church ever since I was wee little, probably from when I was a week old, and this is the first sermon in my memory that is the preaching of the Good News of the Gospel of Christ. He's not preaching about an issue. He's not preaching about a theological position. He's not preaching about anything except this is the Good News. And I thought, wow, this is what I am hungry to hear. This is what I am dying to hear."*

When I read "The Ragamuffin Gospel" years ago, there was a point in which I finally got it. I don't remember exactly what the words were or where it was in the book, but I remember feeling the love of God so clearly and deeply, it was like nothing I had ever experienced before in my life – except perhaps for when I was first saved. That sudden realization that God really does love me in spite of all my ugliness, sinfulness, and downright unloveliness most of the time, and nothing can ever change that!

You can hear this same realization in 1 John 3:1 where John exclaims, *"Behold what manner of love the Father has bestowed on us, that we should be called children of God!"* In Paul's Epistle to the Romans, he practically stops his own discourse and cries out, *"Oh, the depth of the riches both of the wisdom and knowledge of God! How unsearchable are His judgments and His ways past finding out!"* (Romans 11:33). You can almost hear him bursting at the seams, tossing aside his stylus, and jumping up to dance around the room and maybe even shake whoever was there with him.

There's a wideness in God's mercy
*   I cannot find in my own*
And He keeps His fire burning
*   To melt this heart of stone*
Keeps me aching with a yearning
*   Keeps me glad to have been caught*
In the reckless raging fury
*   That they call the love of God*

Our hearts really are like stone most of our lives – even inside many of us Christians – and all too often He has to douse our hearts in flames or smash them with a divine sledge to finally break through to us so we can finally be molded into His vessels. But He rarely breaks us right away; that comes later, but it always comes – of that we can be certain. He loves us too much to leave us where we are, regardless of how content and comfortable we may be.

Sometimes He puts a peculiar ache or unsettledness, a longing deep within us to seek after something more, something much greater...someone like Him. Suddenly, nothing earthly will satisfy our appetite and we have no idea why! That is the start of the journey of faith, the first spark in a great fire He means to kindle within our souls.

As the fire grows and the ice inside our hearts melts, we start to draw closer and closer to Him, and He reveals more of His unfathomable love to us. Before we know it, we're standing before this blazing inferno, and then in the presence of this massive supernova. Yet those are only mere clumsy glimpses of the raging fury of God's love for us!

Now I've seen no band of angels
  But I've heard the soldiers' songs
Love hangs over them like a banner
  Love within them leads them on
To the battle on the journey
  And it's never gonna stop
Ever widening their mercies
  And the fury of His love

There are many banners and labels applied to Christians today, but tragically few of them are related to love. As that traditional children's song declares, the world will know that we are Christians by our love. And this came directly from Jesus Himself Who said in John 13: 35, *"By this all will know that you are My disciples, if you love one another."* Yet where is that love today? Very little of it seems to be in Western Christendom today, even in many of our churches. Perhaps the world is right to accuse us of hypocrisy and all sorts of other evils when it sees how little love we seem to have.

Though the Church may be guilty of many things over the years, the one thing that Jesus will find the most fault in when He judges His churches is our lack of love towards Him, towards our brethren, and towards the world around us. Peter says we are a chosen people, a royal priesthood, and even a holy nation (2 Peter 2: 9-10). And what were we chosen for? To shine the Light of Christ, proclaim His praises, and spread His love to the world around us:

> *"But you are a chosen generation, a royal priesthood, a holy nation, His own special people, that you may proclaim the praises of Him who called you out of darkness into His marvelous light; who once were not a people but are now the people of God, who had not obtained mercy but now have obtained mercy." – 2 Peter 2: 9-10*

If we do not love, we have no right to be called by His Name. We who have obtained mercy are to tell others all about God's incredible mercy and grace.

Joy and sorrow are this ocean
And in their every ebb and flow
Now the Lord a door has opened
That all Hell could never close
Here I'm tested and made worthy
Tossed about but lifted up
In the reckless raging fury
That they call the love of God

Why is this world so rough and this life so difficult, particularly for those who follow hard after God? Doesn't it stand to reason if we are living right and playing by all the rules, shouldn't it be getting better and easier? That sure doesn't seem like much of a good deal if we're trading in our problems for bigger ones and our difficult life for an even harder one. In fact, that really is a pretty poor deal – unless this life is merely the first step in a great eternal journey.

We Christians are here on this earth to be tested, to be refined and purified and purged of our dross. We are here to not only proclaim the love of Christ, but to demonstrate and model His love to those around us. We are not here for our own rest or comfort or dare-I-say-it pleasure – all that comes later when we dwell with Him. So much of this life is about preparing us for the next one, the eternal one. The one that really matters – the one that lasts.

With that in mind, the troubles and sufferings of this life are far more than worth it, as Paul declares in Romans 8:18 and 1 Corinthians 2:9 – *"For I consider that the sufferings of this present time are not worthy to be compared with the glory which shall be revealed in us... Eye has not seen, nor ear heard, nor have entered into the heart of man the things which God has prepared for those who love Him."*

That's the eternal perspective that drives some Christians to not only submit to the flames, but also demand to stack the wood and light the matches themselves. That's the eternal perspective that drives some Christians to demand to be fed to the lions instead of begging to be set free.

That's the eternal perspective that Christ desires each one of us to have.

Walks With Rich

16. The Maker of Noses

*"Christianity is about a daily walk with this person,
Jesus. The heart of Christian faith is a radical and
reasonable trust and focus on Jesus, but for many of us our
focus has shifted very subtly from love for Jesus and
faithfulness to Him and obedience to Him to a set of
doctrines. Life and living come from God - it comes from
Jesus - not from doctrine or good morals. You can be an
utterly moral person and not be alive. Jesus came that we
might have life, not good morals. It's not that I'm opposed to
good morals at all; it's just that sometimes I think we put the
cart before the horse." – Rich Mullins*

At first glance, "The Maker of Noses" seems to be a
rather silly song, but it actually has some pretty deep
meanings to it. This song is about God making each of us
unique, from the peculiar noses on our faces to our dreams
and thoughts and longings. We're not only all special and
unique, we are made in His image for His good pleasure, to
see what we will do with these gifts that He's given to each
of us.

The other part of this song is about finding that paradise
of perfection in which justice and righteousness reigns
supreme. Everyone in the world wants to go there, yet no
one even knows where it is, much less how to get there! If
that place doesn't really exist, then why do we have this
unexplainable yearning for it in the very depths of our souls?
So in our attempts to find that special place we inherently

desire to reach, we follow after our noses and somehow hope we find it.

The Maker of Noses
<u>Isa 8:11-19</u>

I believe there is a place
  Where people live in perfect peace
Where there is food on every plate
  Where work is rewarded and rest is sweet
Where the color of your skin
  Won't get you in or keep you out
Where justice reigns and truth finally wins
  It's hard fought war against fear and doubt

And everyone I know wants to go there too
  But when I ask them how to do it they seem so confused
Do I turn to the left?
  Do I turn to the right?
When I turn to the world they gave me this advice

They said boy you just follow your heart
  But my heart just led me into my chest
They said follow your nose
  But the direction changed every time I went and turned
my head
And they said boy you just follow your dreams
  But my dreams were only misty notions
But the Father of hearts and the Maker of noses
  And the Giver of dreams He's the one I have chosen
And I will follow Him

I believe there'll come a time
  Lord, I pray it's not too far off
There'll be no poverty or crime

There'll be no greed and we will learn how to love
And children will be safe in their homes
And there'll be no violence out on the streets
The old will not be left alone
And the strong will learn how to care for the weak

And everyone I know hopes it comes real soon
But when I ask 'em where I'd find it they seem so
confused
Do I find it in the day?
Do I find it in the night?
When I finally ask the world they give me this advice

Well they said boy you just follow your heart
But my heart just led me into my chest
They said follow your nose
But the direction changed every time I went and turned
my head
And they said boy you just follow your dreams
But my dreams were only misty notions
But the Father of hearts and the Maker of noses
And the Giver of dreams He's the one I have chosen

And oh, I hear the voice of a million dreams
Then I wake in the world that I'm partly made of
And the world that is partly my homemaking
And oh, I hear the song of a heart set free
That will not be kept down
By the fury and sound
Of a world that is wasting away but keeps saying (keeps on
saying)

Saying boy you just follow your heart
But my heart just led me into my chest
They said follow your nose
The direction changed every time I go and turn my head

They said boy you just follow your dreams
But my dreams were only misty notions
But the Father of hearts and the Maker of noses
And the Giver of dreams He's the one I have chosen
And I will follow Him

For as long as I can remember, I've been a dreamer, probably as far back as five or six years old, if not earlier (I just can't remember!). However, I'm not the type that dreams and does nothing about them – when I find something I'm passionate about, I diligently pursue it. For me personally, I think that characteristic came from how I was raised.

Growing up out in the country, there wasn't a whole lot to do after the work was done, so I read books – LOTS of books. We didn't have air-conditioning, so reading close to an open window with a cool breeze blowing in was my thing to do. Even as an adult now, I'll typically read at least a couple dozen books over the course of a year (I'm shooting for 100+ this year). Reading all those books has greatly helped expand my imagination, perspective, and exposed me to a much larger world than I would've ever been able to experience, especially growing up on the farm.

The most formative period of my life wasn't the year before I graduated high school or the months that followed graduation, but the year or two after that when I first ventured out on my own. I remember when I was finishing high school, I began receiving tons of advice and questions about my future and for a while I thought I had it all figured out. But when I went off to college, I quickly found that I wasn't heading anywhere close to where I wanted to be and was going down a road towards a destination that I really didn't want to end up at.

After dropping out of the first college I briefly attended, I spent the better part of the next year figuring out what was really important in life (or at least trying to), where I wanted to go, and what I basically wanted to do. Most would consider that to be a year well-wasted since I was mostly following my nose, but to me that was the most important year of my life (so far). I think that it's better to stop and figure out where you want to go before you rush off marching down just any old road that looks good.

How many people have not taken that precious time to learn about themselves before jumping into college or a career or even most relationships? Isn't it much better to stop and orient yourself before setting off in a certain direction? Isn't it much better to take a few months off or even a year or two between big life transitions to reevaluate your situation and consider your own dreams rather than wake up one day living in a house you don't feel at home in, living in a dead marriage with a big mortgage, and/or daily slaving away in a job you despise?

But what about the issue of eternal destiny and personal salvation? What's the answer to these various dilemmas in life as to the right direction to take? Should we follow our dreams, our hearts, or our noses? And why not? Maybe it's because those feelings and suppositions are all-too-often unreliable and frequently changing. I believe the true answer is to follow after God and let Him direct your paths (Proverbs 3:6). Find out who you are and what you like and dislike, and then define and clarify your dreams. Set out to see your dreams fulfilled, but pursue God first and foremost and He will see to your path.

Instead of bloodying your fists (or head!) on all those doors that God has closed, how about stepping out in faith and following God through the doors that He has opened? Our way through this brief life is really quite simple, if you think about it: pursue God and love Him with all your heart, mind, soul, and strength (Luke 10:27) and He will make your paths straight – or rather, He will reveal where He wants you to go and what He wants you to do next.

146

Sometimes, He wants us to stay right where we are and keep on keeping on, and often those are the times we grow the most in patience, trust, and perseverance.

I believe there'll come a time
  Lord, I pray it's not too far off
There'll be no poverty or crime
  There'll be no greed and we will learn how to love
And children will be safe in their homes
  And there'll be no violence out on the streets
The old will not be left alone
  And the strong will learn how to care for the weak

Someday, there will be perfect peace on this planet, but it won't be by humanity's doing, regardless of how intelligent or clever we may become. Our cumulative knowledge is now doubling every twelve months, yet our problems seem to keep increasing! The fundamental problem on this earth isn't our lack of knowledge, resources, manpower, or money, but that it's fallen and cursed, and since we're part of that problem, we can't even begin to fix it. It's like letting the inmates run the asylum, but on a planetary scale. We need Someone outside this insane-asylum who has the wisdom, power, and authority to put everything in order. And that Someone is Jesus Christ, Who will return to this earth someday and reign in perfect justice, power, and righteousness.

And everyone I know hopes it comes real soon
  But when I ask 'em where I'd find it they seem so confused
Do I find it in the day?
  Do I find it in the night?
When I finally ask the world they give me this advice

This world and all its problems really is a maddening place when you stop and consider it. We all want the same things (generally speaking), but no one has any clue as to how to accomplish it. The best definition of insanity is repeating the same experiment over and over and expecting different results. But since we have no other options that we can accept (as the self-declared rulers of this world), we continue the same experiment and hope it turns out different!

Consider the sheer madness of socialism and communism for a moment. We keep trying the same failed schemes over and over, decade after decade in country after country, and still expect that someday, somehow it'll work. Some of the greatest thinkers in socialism during the last century concluded that the central problem was their own people, so they proceeded to murder as many of them who didn't think like they did as possible. Nothing says communism works quite like slaughtering a couple million of your own people and then calling it progress or liberation. Granted, capitalism isn't perfect, but there aren't nearly as many mass-graves, gulags, and gas-chambers as under the various forms of Marxism.

Well they said boy you just follow your heart
  But my heart just led me into my chest
They said follow your nose
  But the direction changed every time I went and turned my head
And they said boy you just follow your dreams
  But my dreams were only misty notions
But the Father of hearts and the Maker of noses
  And the Giver of dreams He's the one I have chosen
And I will follow Him

The problem with following our dreams – almost as if they are our idols or the sole purpose for living – is that they frequently change. The same can often hold true with following our hearts: it can become an idol. Jeremiah 17:9 says that the heart is deceitful and desperately wicked; that doesn't sound very reliable or trustworthy at all!

The Bible also says to delight yourself in the Lord [first], and [then] He will give you the desires of your heart (Psalm 37:4). Finding genuine fulfillment in this life can really only come from God, and until we realize that and place Him first, all our best efforts are pointless and sheer vanity, a chasing after the wind.

17. Nothing is Beyond You

"He is the image of the invisible God. He is incomprehensible to our western minds - as He was to eastern ones. He came from that beyond that no human mind as visited. When we try to squeeze Him into our systems of thought, He vanishes - He slips through our grasp and then reappears and (in so many words) says, 'No man takes My life from Me. No man forces his will on Me. I am not yours to handle and cheapen. You are Mine to love and make holy."
– Rich Mullins

This song is from "The Jesus Record/Demos" and is mostly a paraphrase of the first section of Psalm 139, which is about God knitting us together and watching us over the course of our lives. God sees everything throughout all Creation, and as the pinnacle of His handiwork, His eyes are always upon us. There's nowhere in this vast universe we can escape His sight of us; Adam and Eve tried, as did Cain and countless others. Just as every child has tried to hide from their parents at one time or another, so all of us have tried to hide from God in our own way.

The other mantra of this song is that nothing is impossible for God – not even redeeming fallen, sinful people to Himself. Though with men such things are impossible, nothing is impossible for God (Matthew 19:6). No matter how bitter your heart is, no matter how unworthy you may feel, and no matter what you've done, you're never too far away or too far gone for God to reach you.

150

Nothing is Beyond You
Psalm 42:7-8; Psalm 93; Psalm 139:1-12; 1 Cor 15:51-57; 2
Cor 5:21; Rev 1:8; Rev 22:13

Where could I go, where could I run
Even if I found the strength to fly
And if I rose on the wings of the dawn
And crashed through the corner of the sky

If I sailed past the edge of the sea
Even if I made my bed in Hell
Still there You would find me

'Cause nothing is beyond You
You stand beyond the reach
Of our vain imaginations
Our misguided piety
The heavens stretch to hold You
And deep cries out to deep
Singing that nothing is beyond You
Nothing is beyond You

Time cannot contain You
You fill eternity
Sin can never stain You
Death has lost its sting

And I cannot explain the way You came to love me
Except to say that nothing is beyond You
Nothing is beyond You

If I should shrink back from the light
So I can sink into the dark
If I take cover and I close my eyes

151

Even then You would see my heart

And You'd cut through all my pain and rage
The darkness is not dark to You
And night's as bright as day

Nothing is beyond You
You stand beyond the reach
Of our vain imaginations
Our misguided piety
The heavens stretch to hold You
And deep cries out to deep
Singing that nothing is beyond You
Nothing is beyond You

And time cannot contain You
You fill eternity
Sin can never stain You
And death has lost its sting

And I cannot explain the way You came to love me
Except to say that nothing is beyond You
Nothing is beyond You
Nothing is beyond You

Often the idea of God seeing everything we do can be quite unsettling, especially when we want to just be left alone and indulge in something that we really shouldn't. It's one thing to cheat on your diet, but quite another to cheat on your taxes, your work – or even your spouse. The knowledge that God sees everything we do should keep us from being too quick to cheat, lie, and steal, but it can also become a terrible burden on us – if we have the wrong view of God.

Years ago, the late Dr. Chuck Smith of Calvary Chapel told the story about how one of his grandchildren came to him once rather worried and sheepishly asked, "Does God watch me all the time?" The child was very concerned because he'd been told that God watches everything you do – especially when you're bad. Pastor Smith took the boy in his arms and said, "Well, it's true. God really does watch you all the time – but it's because He loves you so much that He cannot take His eyes off of you!" I imagine that he hugged him tightly and then his grandson scampered away with a huge smile on his face, and that's the reaction I believe that God has with each one of us.

What an incredible difference that simple truth can make in our relationship with God! Does God watch over us for good or evil? Since God is good, there is only one right answer. Who created love in the first place? Wasn't it God? And doesn't it stand to reason that if we have the ability to love, then doesn't our Creator? When we watch our own children, don't we watch them out of love and concern, not in order to catch them in wrongdoing just so we can punish them? What sort of wicked parent watches over their own children for evil? Yet that's how much of the world views God!

How we react to the knowledge that God watches everything we do can tell us much about how we personally view and perceive God. If we react with fear and resentment to God's ever-watchful gaze upon us, we likely have an unloving and unbiblical view of God, as if He's always harsh, capricious, and quick to anger. However, if we understand God's basic character and accept that God really does love us, we won't have those same fears because we know that God is watching us for good, not evil.

Nothing is beyond You
   You stand beyond the reach
Of our vain imaginations
   Our misguided piety
The heavens stretch to hold You

And deep cries out to deep
Singing that nothing is beyond You
   Nothing is beyond You

When you stop and think about God and how much He
hates sin, it really is unexplainable not only why God loves
us, but the incredible, furious nature of His love. Imagine the
patience He must have to watch us keep falling down over
and over for years and still faithfully helping us to our feet,
even though He knows we'll fall right back down in a few
minutes (or seconds!). Imagine being the mother or father of
a small toddler for not just a mere year or so, but for decades
and for billions of people all at the same time!

Yet that's what makes Him God: His reckless, raging,
furious love for us in spite of how much we hurt Him.

Where could I go, where could I run
   Even if I found the strength to fly
And if I rose on the wings of the dawn
   And crashed through the corner of the sky

If I sailed past the edge of the sea
   Even if I made my bed in Hell
Still there You would find me

So many of us spend all our lives (or most of them)
running from God, but He is faithful to outrun us and wait
for us, like those old Looney Tune cartoons with Sam the
Sheepdog and Ralph the Wolf. Wherever you're running to,
God is already there waiting for you, no matter how long or
how far you've run! You can't escape Him, so why keep
trying to? Repent of your sins, humble yourself, accept His
free gift of salvation, and just embrace Him!

If I should shrink back from the light
   So I can sink into the dark

If I take cover and I close my eyes
Even then You would see my heart

Our flesh craves darkness, and each of us has our very own shadow-self that we must guard against and often battle. As Jesus said in John 3:18-21 – *"He who believes in Him is not condemned; but he who does not believe is condemned already, because he has not believed in the name of the only begotten Son of God. And this is the condemnation, that the light has come into the world, and men loved darkness rather than light, because their deeds were evil. For everyone practicing evil hates the light and does not come to the light, lest his deeds should be exposed. But he who does the truth comes to the light, that his deeds may be clearly seen, that they have been done in God."*
One of my deepest fears is that my love for God will grow cold someday and that I'll shrink or even turn away from Him. I've watched it happen to others several times, even people I thought were rock-solid in their faith. I've seen the love of some not only fade into numbness, but keep going and later turn to rabid hatred towards God. What's worse: the sudden cataclysm that causes you to doubt God or the slow, almost undetectable slide into the death of the relationship? With the former, there's often a return once the time of testing has ended. But with the latter, the decision to walk away from God has been made repeatedly in a million different ways and times, and it often becomes permanent.

And You'd cut through all my pain and rage
The darkness is not dark to You
And night's as bright as day

Before I became a Christian, there was a period towards the end of high school where I was rather bitter and angry towards God, though I had no idea why – nor did I have any reason to be. But I was still angry with Him nevertheless, and the way that expressed itself was by me lashing out against "organized religion" (i.e., Christianity) and the Church. I was upset for no reason and that seemed to be a decent scapegoat, probably because my parents were Christians and I wanted nothing to do with it.

But after I was broken and became saved, all that anger just vanished and was replaced by love. It was like I was aimlessly stumbling around in the dark and kept bumping into the walls, and then He shined this brilliant light into the room and all the darkness (and frustration and anger) just vanished. He set me free and gave my life purpose and meaning and direction – and all I had to do the entire time was just turn to Him and accept what He offered.

Walks With Rich

18. The Other Side of the World

"A faith that moves mountains is a faith that expands horizons. It does not bring us into a smaller world full of easy answers, but into a larger one where there is room for wonder." – Rich Mullins

Every day when I skim the news, it seems that the world is getting smaller and smaller. In the age of the Internet, instant communications, and supersonic travel, events happening on the other side of the world often feel like they're practically down the street. But I've discovered that when I unplug for a few days, the world seems to quickly expand – especially if I'm traveling and don't have access to a vehicle that I can quickly get around in!

"The Other Side of the World" is about God building His Kingdom all across the world, the Kingdom of the Redeemed, the Ecclesia – the "Called-out Ones." Though our days seem to be growing darker and more tumultuous, even to the point when our hearts may fail us for fear of what's happening, God is not worried at all (Psalm 2, Proverbs 3:24-26). He is steadily working out His plans for this world – building His Church, gathering the scattered remnants of Israel back to their ancient homeland, and setting the world stage for the establishment of His Kingdom on earth when Christ returns to reign and rule.

The Other Side of the World

Isa 11:1-9; Hab 2:4; Matt 18:23-25; Rom 9:16-24; 1 Peter
2:4-9; Rev 7:9-10, Rev 12:10-12

Well the other side of the world
 Is not so far away as I thought that it was
As I thought that it was so far away
 But the other side of the world
Is not so far away
 And the distance just dissolves into the love
Into the love

And the New Jerusalem won't be as easy to build
 As I hoped it would be
As I hoped it would be easy to build
 But the New Jerusalem won't be so easy to build
There's many bellies to fill and many hearts to free
 Got to set them free

But I see a people who've learned to walk in faith
 With mercy in their hearts
And glory on their faces
 And I can see the people
And I pray it won't be long
 Until Your kingdom comes

And I know that the gates of hell
 Are not prone to prevail
As I thought that they were
 As I once thought they were prone to prevail
But I know that the gates of Hell
 They have been destined to fail
I see Satan impaled on the sword of the Word
 On the sword of the Word

And I see the people who have learned to walk in faith
 With mercy in their hearts

And glory on their faces
  And I can see the people
And I pray it won't be long
  Until Your kingdom comes

And I can see the people who have learned to walk in faith
  With mercy in their hearts
And glory on their faces
  And I can see the people
And I pray it won't be long
  Until Your kingdom comes
The other side of the world

Our brief time here on this earth is not about how high we ended up in society or how much stuff we managed to accumulate, but how closely we walked with God. Did we walk by sight as the countless masses do, or did we learn to genuinely walk by faith? How well did we love others, especially those who are rather unlovable?

Did we show – and not merely just tell – others of the great mercy, grace, and love of God that we ourselves have been given? Did we use the many talents that we have been given to the best of our abilities? Did we use our gifts for our own glory or for God's glory? Did we grow the Kingdom by our love of God and those around us – even our enemies?

Well the other side of the world
  Is not so far away as I thought that it was
As I thought that it was so far away
  But the other side of the world
Is not so far away
  And the distance just dissolves into the love
Into the love

Though the world is a very big place, our modern age has made it feel quite small these days. And though cultures can be radically different from one another, we're all still made in God's image and all have similar, fundamental characteristics. We all have dreams and desires, and we all need love, grace, and forgiveness. We all need to know that there is a God who loves us more than we can possibly imagine, and that He yearns for us to come into His Family.

And the New Jerusalem won't be as easy to build
  As I hoped it would be
As I hoped it would be easy to build
  But the New Jerusalem won't be so easy to build
There's many bellies to fill and many hearts to free
  Got to set them free

There are some sights that we see which will be forever imprinted in our minds, like when we first see our newborn baby, that instant those chapel doors open and we see our soon-to-be spouse, and that last moment the coffin bearing our loved one is lowered into the earth. Each of us have our own special moments that are emblazoned in our mind's eye, and one of those for me is when I caught my first glimpse of the Old City of Jerusalem from the Mount of Olives.

The bus wound its way up the ridge past Hebrew University and "The Holy City" song by Stephen Adams was playing through the speakers, and then suddenly there it was: the Temple Mount surrounded by the limestone walls and crowned with the golden Dome of the Rock. The only way the sight could've been greater would be if the Jewish Temple stood there in all its glory – and some day it will. Below the Old City ran the Kidron Valley and just below us were the tens of thousands of limestone tombs, while in the distant background were dozens of construction cranes, Israel's national "bird."

The New Jerusalem mentioned here conjures up pictures of the City of God that descends to earth at the end of Revelation, the Bride of Christ. With every soul that repents and calls upon the name of the Lord, the kingdom of Heaven is built. Brick by brick, stone by stone, and person by person. One day the Church will be complete and taken up to Christ, and then we will dwell with Him forever.

And I know that the gates of hell
  Are not prone to prevail
As I thought that they were
  As I once thought they were prone to prevail
But I know that the gates of Hell
  They have been destined to fail
I see Satan impaled on the sword of the Word
  On the sword of the Word

Though history continues to march towards the Tribulation (or the Seventieth Week of Daniel), to the time in which all Hell will be turned loose on earth, God remains in complete control – no matter what happens on this earth. He is completely sovereign over everything in all Creation. One day when the world reaches its darkest day, Jesus Christ will return to this earth, slay His enemies, and imprison Satan for a thousand years. It's literally set in stone – in the unbreakable Word of God – and it's going to happen as sure as the sun will rise tomorrow morning.

When I first became a Christian, accepting the Word was more about the inner transformation of my heart rather than really being convinced of it in my head. That change didn't occur until about four years later, when I decided that since I've been a Christian for a while, I should probably get my act together and read the Bible for myself and really see what I've gotten myself into. I still had some rather muddied-up beliefs about science, particularly concerning the Theory of Evolution. I started reading a couple of Josh

McDowell books and became convinced in my head that Jesus really was the Messiah and that the historical accounts in the Bible were indeed true – but I was still very ignorant about what else was in it.

So I started asking some tough (and sometimes trivial) questions about the world and digging into the Bible and learning about different perspectives concerning a wide variety of subjects such as Israel, the Jewish people, race issues, the End Times, Evolution/Creation, dinosaurs, and the Ice Age. After a few months of poking and studying, I became convinced that the entirety of the Bible is true, and that only that Book has the accurate account of the past and also the true prophetic picture of the future. Isaiah 46:9-11 declares that God is unique and alone knows the End from the Beginning (and every moment in between!).

One study that was particularly helpful was Chuck Missler's "Learn the Bible in 24 Hours" series, in which he surveyed the entire Bible from the perspective of a systems engineer and demonstrated that the Bible is one integrated message from God to us. He digs into all these different details that are often overlooked and shows that when taken literally and seriously, the Bible alone – because it's the Word of God – gives an accurate history of how the different peoples and nations came about, the different "ages" and geological features of the earth, describes why the world is the way it is today, and predicts the future of Israel and the nations around her.

When you stop and actually think about some of the current global political issues today (namely Israel), the shoe starts to pinch a little tight. For example, why have the Jews been singled out for persecution throughout most of recorded history? How is that Israel has been restored as a nation – and with their original language no less – and Jews from all over the world are regathering there, just as the Bible predicted more than 2,500 years ago? Why is the entire world – including most democratic nations – turning

163

against Israel though she is the only real democracy in the Middle East? Why is Jerusalem – an isolated city with no real economic or geopolitical value – the focus of so much of the news today?

How is it that Israel is not only surviving despite the incredible odds against her, but thriving such that they're one of the primary suppliers of flowers and citrus to Europe, even though the entire land was barren and covered with malaria-filled swamps and arid deserts less than sixty years ago? How is it that Israel is a military, technology, and medical giant not only in the Middle East, but in the world? As Benjamin Disraeli once told the Queen of England, the mere survival of the Jew is one of the best evidences for God. Israel is God's prophetic timepiece, and His clock is ticking along precisely as foretold in the Bible.

And then there are all the geological, chronological, and scientific problems between the Evolutionists and the Creationists. What about the dozens of limiting factors that strongly indicate the world is less than 100,000 years old, with many indicating it's less than 10,000 years old? If mankind has been evolving for millions of years, then where are all the bodies? And that's just for man, not all the other thousands upon thousands of species! How can there be such huge fossil-graveyards full of creatures from the different epochs all jumbled together and out of order? How can you have fossilized jellyfish and other very fragile, soft-tissue organisms that appear to have been instantly mineralized? If the dinosaurs died out 65+ million years ago, why are we finding frozen dinosaur bones with fresh blood and marrow still in them? Where are all the transitional forms that Darwin postulated that must exist for his theory to have a leg to stand on? Where is even one valid transitional form? There should be literally millions! Why have the Evolutionists recently departed from long ages of slow, gradual change to long ages of nearly instantaneous change? Could it be that they changed their tune because of lack of evidence (which is quite embarrassing to any theory)? When I was in elementary school, a frog turning into a prince was a fairy-tale – but now it's practically accepted science!

Those were just a few of the many questions I started asking years ago, and then I searched out the truth wherever I could find it. For me personally, the only worldview that can adequately answer all those questions is the Judeo-Christian worldview as proclaimed in the Bible. All the other views don't even come close and usually fall apart under basic scrutiny.

And I see the people who have learned to walk in faith
*   With mercy in their hearts*
And glory on their faces
*   And I can see the people*
And I pray it won't be long
*   Until Your kingdom comes*

Though this verse speaks of believers being called out of the world, I often picture the remnants of the Jews stumbling out of the Nazi death-camps after being liberated and then arriving in Israel shortly afterwards, the second regathering of the Jews to the Promised Land. From the ashes of the Holocaust, the Jewish nation was reborn – and has miraculously survived. The day after it was founded on May 14, 1948, Israel was attacked by five Arab armies on all three borders. In those early days of the war, the times were so desperate that the immigrants were immediately given rifles and pressed into military service upon leaving the boats: "Welcome to Israel – now go fight for her!" Israel had no navy, a crop-duster and three pilots for an air force, and a ragtag military that was still being organized – yet they not only survived, they enlarged their territory. How was that possible? Because God fought on their behalf as He promised. The DVD series "Against All Odds – Israel Survives" documents many of these recent miracles in His

165

land. One of the more recent ones in the last few years is Hamas complaining that "Their god redirects our rockets!"

It's been said that God is the "God of Second Chances," and that couldn't be more true with regards to Israel. In fact, that truth is scattered all throughout the Bible from its earliest pages. One of the more interesting passages to consider is Stephen's address to the Sanhedrin in Acts 7. If you read it closely, you can see that his main point is that Israel always disobeys God the first time but then obeys Him the second. Abraham was called to go to the Promised Land from Ur, but only moved upriver to Haran before being called a second time, which he then heeded. Joseph was only accepted by his brothers the second time, Moses was accepted by his people after the second time, the Israelites accepted the second set of Ten Commandments, the second generation of the Israelites entered the Promised Land, and Israel only turned from idolatry the second time after entering the land after the Babylonian Captivity.

The last point that Stephen didn't get a chance to make before he was martyred was that the Jews had rejected their Messiah the first time, but they would accept Him the second time – the time that appears to be quickly approaching. And what is happening in our day? The Second Regathering of Israel to the Promised Land from all over the world as foretold in Ezekiel 36-37, Leviticus 26, Isaiah 11:11-12, and several other passages. Throughout Deuteronomy the history of Israel was described in detail by Moses even before they entered the land, from their conquering of the land to their prosperity and disobedience, to the Diaspora and then eventual regathering from all over the world. There are even hints of the Holocaust and horrible persecution in the cursings of chapter 28, along with the promise to regather them to the land if they repented and sought Him.

That's probably one of the reasons I love visiting Israel so much: you can go there and literally watch dozens of ancient prophecies being fulfilled. They are rebuilding the desolate cities, digging up the ruins of their forefathers, they are prospering as never before and even making the desert bloom! Granted, none of it's been easy for them, and it's through their decades of tough sacrifice and blood, sweat, and tears that Israel is being restored. But none of it would be possible without God watching over them, protecting them, and nurturing His tiny nation once again. Leviticus 26 and other passages proclaim that the land of Israel won't be fruitful for anyone other than the Jews, which is precisely what we see throughout history. The land of Palestine was absolutely barren and worthless to the Arabs and all the other nations that conquered it – until the Jews returned and the land began to thrive and blossom again.

In our day and age, Christianity seems to be failing, especially in the West. It appears to be very weak, fickle, faltering, and seems so quick to compromise with the world. After nearly two thousand years, much of the organized church feels tired, worn out, and on the surface appears to have made very little difference on this messed up planet. But among our congregations, there is the true Church, the small body of believers who are completely sold out for Christ, who have banked everything on Him and are shining His light into the world around them. Those are the fertile soils that Christ says will produce yields of 30, 60, 100, or greater. Those are the sheep who hear His voice and follow Him wherever He goes.

No matter how dark this world gets, God is working out His plan in this Age of Grace. One by one, He is calling out a peculiar people to Himself and bringing them into His Family. In fact, He is bringing more people into the Kingdom now than ever before in history! Our Lord will continue to build His Church and see it to completion, and no one and nothing can ever hinder that!

19. Ready for the Storm

*"God calls us to 'be strong' and we mistake that for a call
to omnipotence. We confuse strength to endure trials with an
ability to walk unfrustrated through life. We convince
ourselves that if we were strong we would never fail, never
tire, never hurt, never need. We begin to measure strength in
terms of ease of progress, equate power with success,
endurability with invincibility and inevitably, when our
illusions of omnipotence is shattered, we condemn ourselves
for being weak." – Rich Mullins*

"Ready for the Storm" is written from the perspective of a
sailor on a ship in the midst of a raging storm. Picture that
sailor lashed to the rigging and bracing for the next swell to
crash over the side and pummel him. Imagine the winds and
waves roaring and the sailor hanging on for dear life because
that's all he can do. He's made himself ready for the storm as
much as he could, and now he has to cling to whatever he
can no matter what the winds and waves throw at him.

Though the storm is terrible, that sailor knows that the
seas will calm and the skies will clear sooner or later. All he
has to do is make it through one more wave and keep his
faith. And then make it through the next one…

Ready for the Storm
Isaiah 50:5-11

The waves crash in the tide rolls out
It's an angry sea but there is no doubt
That the lighthouse will keep shining out
To warn a lonely sailor
And the lightning strikes
And the wind cuts cold
Through the sailor's bones
Through the sailor's soul
'Til there's nothing left that he can hold
Except a rolling ocean

Oh I am ready for the storm
Yes sir ready
I am ready for the storm
I'm ready for the storm

Oh give me mercy for my dreams
'Cause every confrontation seems to tell me
What it really means
To be this lonely sailor
And when the sky begins to clear
The sun it melts away my fear
And I shed a silent weary tear
For those who mean to love me

Oh I am ready for the storm
Yes sir ready
I am ready for the storm
I'm ready for the storm

The distance it is no real friend
And time will take its time
And you will find that in the end
It brings you me
This lonely sailor
And when You take me by the hand

And You love me, Lord, You love me
And I should have realized
I had no reasons to be frightened

Oh I am ready for the storm
Yes sir ready
I am ready for the storm
Yes sir ready
I am ready for the storm
Yes sir ready
I am ready for the storm
I'm ready for the storm

This life is often full of terrible, raging storms – and it's not IF those storms come, as much as WHEN they come – of that we can be certain. Sometimes the waves are so huge and furious that we fear we can't possibly survive another one, and all we can do is hang on for dear life and hope we live through it. Sometimes the lightning strikes so closeby and so suddenly that we fear we'll be struck dead, but the Lord has promised to be faithful and bring us through every one of life's storms. Yes, we will probably be bruised, battered, and even broken on this long voyage, but He has promised to bring us safely into the harbor.

After moving to Florida the year after graduating high school, the first major hurricane I experienced was Hurricane Andrew in 1992, and it was one of the worst in American history. Though I was a few hundred miles north of where it actually struck, I'll never forget the winds and waves that relentlessly pounded the coast, and then all the newscasts of the devastation in South Florida afterwards. In Ohio, we had bad thunderstorms and tornadoes to contend with, but never a hurricane like that!

The morning after most of the rains had ended, the wind was still howling and the swells were bigger than I'd ever seen before. And since the worst was over and the waves were still huge, there was only one thing for a nineteen year-old to do: go surfing. There were a handful of us out there, and the waves were such that we spent more time paddling and trying to get past the whitecaps than actually surfing, but it was still a great experience. I had never felt such raw power like that before, and I figured that it would be a once-in-a-lifetime experience (and it was!). In hindsight, going out on the ocean that morning probably wasn't such a great idea, but I did love the experience – and I did live to tell about it!

Of all the times I have been out on the ocean, that was the only one where I really felt afraid. I had this tangible feeling that I could get hit by the wrong wave and simply not come back up, or at least not come back up breathing. The fear was very real that day, and I remember praying that God would protect me, even though I was doing something quite risky and foolish. I've never been much for adrenaline-highs, but I was that morning.

Did you know that being afraid or knowing fear is something that God cannot experience? Theologically, since God is perfect, holy, omnipotent, and omniscient, God cannot fear and can never be surprised. He cannot ever act contrary to His own nature. He cannot lie (Titus 1:2), He cannot sin (James 1:13), and He cannot ever be anything other than perfect. Since God is all-powerful and all-knowing, He cannot even worry because it would violate His nature.

Over and over in the Bible, He commands us not to fear or be afraid. In fact, just about every time He or one of His angelic servants appears before someone in the Scriptures, He commands them to not be afraid. Jesus said not to even worry about much of life at all (Matthew 6:25-34). Most people think that the opposite of love is hate, but that would not be accurate, at least as far as the Bible is concerned. The raw emotions of love and hate may be contrary to one another, but the opposite of genuine love is fear, which often triggers the other emotions such as hate, anger, and anxiety:

There is no fear in love; but perfect love casts out fear, because fear involves torment. But he who fears has not been made perfect in love…For God has not given us a spirit of fear, but of power and of love and of a sound mind. (1 John 4:18; 2 Timothy 1:7)

The more we really trust God with our lives and our hearts, the less fear and anxiety we should have. It's easy to worry when life flies apart at the seams and flips your world upside down. It's easy to get discouraged and lose heart when life continues throwing you curveballs and nothing ever seems to be working out very well. It's easy to build thick walls around your heart after someone you've trusted for a long time completely betrays you and wounds you to the very core of your being. It's easy to fear just about anything, but it's hard to trust – but that's what God calls us to.

Faith and trust walk hand in hand, and one cannot be had without the other. Where there is genuine faith, trust is there also. The funny thing is that so many of us easily trust God with our eternal destiny, yet worry about the tiniest other things. He wants us to trust Him with everything, even the little details about what to wear, what to eat, and every other seemingly insignificant detail of our lives.

As for the sudden storms we'll go through from time to time, when a storm is raging at sea, the sailors batten down the hatches and secure themselves below decks. When a storm is raging on the coast and on land, the people board up all the windows and hunker down somewhere safe. Well, unless they're crazy and rather foolish, then they booze up and throw a hurricane-party! Or they just wait and then go surfing.

But what are we as Christians to do when life's storms are raging and threatening to devastate us? We can prepare for the storm by staying grounded in the Word and in prayer. We are to take regular inventory and stock of our lives and those around us and remain close to the Lord. But when the storm is really raging, we must hang onto the Lord for dear life and rely upon Him to bring us through it.

Make no mistake, my friend – know for certain that the storms will come sooner or later! The storms that began in my own life recently were a long time coming, and I was not prepared. I didn't even have time to lash myself to the rigging! But God has been faithful and has carried me through. Daily dig into the Word and grow closer to the Lord not only when the skies are clouding over, but when they're clear and sunny. Hold fast to your faith and never, ever let go!

20. Sometimes by Step

"The biggest problem with life is that it's just daily. You can never get so healthy that you don't have to continue to eat right. Because every day I have to make the right choices about what I eat and how much exercise I need. Spiritually we're in much the same place. I go on these binges where it's like 'I'm going to memorize the five books of Moses.' I expect to be able to live off the momentum. The only thing that praying today is good for is today. So, with [the songs] 'Step by Step' and 'Sometimes by Step,' it's not what you did, and not what you say you're going to do, it's what you do today." – Rich Mullins

"Sometimes by Step" is a beautiful contemporary praise song often sung in church services years after it was released. A companion song is "Step by Step," which is shorter and more praise-oriented, the main difference being that "Step by Step" doesn't contain the two verses, just the chorus. The chorus of both are particularly moving when sung by an entire church at once, especially when sung acapella.

This song is a great reminder to keep everything in perspective. Like Abraham, we are sojourners and characters in this incredible story of faith that God has been writing for the last six thousand years (or rather, all eternity past). We are people of faith on this Road to Righteousness, and the only way we can get there is by daily walking with God step by step, step by step.

Sometimes by Step
Gen 15:5-6; Psalm 63; Isa 30:21; Rom 9:8; Heb 12:1-3

Sometimes the night was beautiful
Sometimes the sky was so far away
Sometimes it seemed to stoop so close
You could touch it but your heart would break

Sometimes the morning came too soon
Sometimes the day could be so hot
There was so much work left to do
But so much You'd already done

Oh God, You are my God
And I will ever praise You
Oh God, You are my God
And I will ever praise You
I will seek You in the morning
And I will learn to walk in Your ways
And step by step You'll lead me
And I will follow You all of my days

Sometimes I think of Abraham
How one star he saw had been lit for me
He was a stranger in this land
And I am that, no less than he

And on this road to righteousness
Sometimes the climb can be so steep
I may falter in my steps
But never beyond Your reach

Oh God, You are my God
And I will ever praise You

Oh God, You are my God
And I will ever praise You
I will seek You in the morning
And I will learn to walk in Your ways
And step by step You'll lead me
And I will follow You all of my days

In our lives, so many of us frequently want to rush ahead and zip right to that finish line or onto the next phase or event. However, reaching that goal line isn't necessarily what may be most important to God. To Him, every tiny step we take along the way is most important, living one day at a time. It's the journey that really matters to Him, not the solely the destination because that's already set. It's our daily walk that prepares us for His Kingdom, not merely when we die.

Whenever I get out of the habit of running and then get back into it, the first few weeks are absolutely miserable. I'm sore, out of breath, whiny, and wonder why I'm even doing this in the first place. But then as I get more into shape and start stretching and stressing those muscles, the stronger I become and the further I can run.

As a software developer, I've observed the same law, but for the mind rather than the body. It's not in the easy days that I become a better engineer, but in the ones where I really get stuck and pound my head against the wall for a few hours and sometimes even days! Often just when I think I've run out of tricks up my sleeve, I'll stumble upon a new path and head down that for a while. Sooner or later, the problem is solved (or mitigated) and then I'm on to the next one. But even though I solved the problem, where did my growth as a developer really occur? In those stressful, frustrating hours I was fumbling and stumbling around, long before the solution presented itself. And yes, God has helped me fix bugs at times…

The same holds true for our hearts and our personal growth towards God. It's not in the normal, predictable days when most of our deepest growth occurs, but in the times of trial, those dark days when we slip down to the very end of our rope, tie a knot, and hang on for dear life. Most people tend to think that growth occurs in slow, steady increments, but in reality it doesn't – it occurs in fits and spurts, in highs and lows.

Do we somehow magically become "kingdom material" when we finally cross the finish line or get to the other side of the river into Eternity? No – we gradually become molded in His image every step along the journey. He's growing us, stretching us, and maturing us with every decision we make and every day we wake, and that's the entire purpose of the journey. It's so easy to get caught up in worrying about the future when all we should be wondering is whether we're obeying God at that particular moment or not. Step by step, breath by breath, God is reshaping us and bringing us into His Kingdom.

The first time I really heard this song was when I was pulling into the parking lot at my job in Palo Alto, the "brain-trust" of Silicon Valley. For whatever reason, the song resonated within me and I had to just stop and listen to it. Then the tears started pouring out and the intense praying came. The culture of the high-tech company I was working for was rather antagonistic towards Christians by the nature of their business (casino video-gaming machines), and sometimes it wasn't very easy working there. Most of the people were nice and cordial, but let's just say there was no love lost on the Church or Christians within the company.

So there I am sitting in my car in the parking lot bawling my eyes out over this song, hoping that no one will see me and start asking really awkward questions, and then it hits me – what does it matter? This company will come and go (which it did two years later), but my relationship with my

King will last for all eternity! He is my God and I will follow
Him all of my days, and nothing can ever change that!

Sometimes I think of Abraham
   How one star he saw had been lit for me
He was a stranger in this land
   And I am that, no less than he

When I hear this verse, I can't help thinking that God has
His own divine "star registry" that has each of our names
inscribed on a particular star. Sometimes I like to look up to
the heavens and ponder which one God has set aside just for
me (so to speak)! Back in Genesis when Lot separated
himself away from Abraham and God called His friend
aside, He told him to look up to the heavens and know for
certain that his descendants would be as numerous as the
stars in the sky – if he could count them! All we who are
friends of God and have placed our faith in Him are counted
among those very same stars that Abraham saw that night –
stars innumerable!

As time goes on in this world and I see more that there is
to see and learn more about life, the more I see that we
people of faith are just passing through, that this is not our
home. We are sojourners here on this earth, the proverbial
strangers in a strange land. And the closer we grow to the
Lord, the more strangers to this world we become. What a
comfort it is to know that this place is not all there is for us,
that we really don't belong here, and that God has our
perfect Home warm and waiting for us.

And on this road to righteousness
   Sometimes the climb can be so steep
I may falter in my steps
   But never beyond Your reach

I personally love the phrase "road to righteousness" because that's our very own yellow-brick road to the Emerald City of Christ. It's the way of sanctification and being daily remade to be just a little more like Him. But what awaits us is no charlatan hiding behind a curtain or a wanna-be wizard, but the one and only King of the entire universe, and He's invited us to the most incredible wedding feast of all time!

Along this Road to Righteousness, from time to time we will stumble and we will fall, but God is faithful to bring us to Himself no matter what. When most of us arrive in Heaven, we're going to be pretty broken, bruised, and beaten up. And then He'll fix all of us up real good and invite us to supper, and then after we're stuffed and satisfied, He'll welcome us into our eternal rest with Him.

Oh God, You are my God
And I will ever praise You
Oh God, You are my God
And I will ever praise You
I will seek You in the morning
And I will learn to walk in Your ways
And step by step You'll lead me
And I will follow You all of my days

There's something very special about worshipping God first thing in the morning, even when you're still sort of sleepy and half-awake. Maybe it's about being fresh and unburdened before all the demands of the day start sweeping you away, and being able to seek after God with a clear head and a fresh heart. There's a certain soothing calmness about reading and praying in the morning when the house is quiet and everyone's still asleep. Though I don't always meet with Him as consistently as I'd like to in the morning, I personally love meeting Him just before the sun comes up, when there's hot coffee nearby and the day starts to awaken.

So much of our journey on this Road to Righteousness is about simply learning to follow Him wherever He may lead us, being faithful, and learning to just trust Him and walk in His ways. His path for us isn't always very smooth, and often the Road is full of twists, turns, and potholes, but He never promised it would be easy and carefree. He only promised to mold us to Himself and bring us into His Kingdom.

Walks With Rich

21. Waiting

"And I'm all the time being asked by people, 'How do you feel closer to God?' And I kinda always want to say, 'I don't know.' When I read the lives of most of the great saints, they didn't necessarily feel very close to God. When I read the Psalms, I get the feeling like David and the other psalmists felt very far from God for most of the time. Closeness to God is not about feelings. Closeness to God is about obedience. It's just as simple as that." – Rich Mullins

"Waiting" is about just what the name implies: waiting on God. We wait on God to do so many different things in our lives – we wait on Him to speak or move or change someone or just fix our difficult situation. And don't think that asking for patience is going to help speed things along, because if God really answers your prayer literally, then you might be waiting much, much longer!

Waiting on the Lord and having patience seems to be an integral part of faith, particularly the Judeo-Christian faith. After all, we Christians have been waiting for Jesus to return for the last two thousand years, while our Jewish brothers and sisters have been waiting to see the prophetic fulfillment of the Scriptures for much, much longer. Sometimes it seems like the End Times are just around the corner, while other days they may feel like many decades away.

Patience and prayer are more about changing our own hearts and limited perspectives than having something else happen – both are about our own internal battles than our external circumstances. A big part of learning patience and contentment is about us forcing ourselves to just settle down and wait on Him, and so often that is the hardest thing to do. Everything within our human nature wants to seize the reins and start lashing those horses in front of us until we get back on whatever track we think we should be on. Meanwhile, God is there shaking His Head and saying, "Trust Me!" or "Just be patient a little while longer!"

Waiting
1 Cor 15:51-58; 1 John 2:28-3:3

Stand on the corner, I watch my breath freeze in the air
See how it lifts and then vanishes
But I know You're still there
Well, I've got nowhere else to go
'Cause the only life that I know comes from You

And I can't walk away
Though the truth is that it can be so hard to wait
When a million voices whisper,
And they tell me I should leave
Into the shadows that the moon casts
On these alleys and these streets
But I know that chasing shadows won't get me anywhere
'Cause I've been there

So I stand on the promise,
'Cause I know that the promise is sure
That it comes from beyond us and tells us again
That there's a whole 'nother world
Well, the one I'm in keeps spinning 'round
But I want to stay right here 'cause I found You

And I can't walk away

Though the truth is that it can be so hard to wait
When a million voices whisper,
  And they tell me I should leave
Into the shadows that the moon casts
  On these alleys and these streets
But I know that chasing shadows won't get me anywhere
  'Cause I've been there

So I'm waiting for You Jesus
  'Cause I know that those who wait
They will mount with wings like eagles
  They will run and not grow faint
They will walk and not grow weary
  Their strength will be renewed
Coming from You

So I wait
  I'm waiting for You
Waiting for You
  So come back soon
I'm waiting for You

Though I've probably listened to this song hundreds of times over the years, it never really meant much to me until after my marriage hit the rocks. I found myself in this very uncomfortable situation where I couldn't go forward and I certainly couldn't go back; all I could do was wait upon the Lord for Him to do something. And that waiting unleashed an entirely new set of lessons that I had never had to learn before.

Patience does not come easy to me – it never has. To my credit (or detriment, depending on the perspective), I have prayed for patience before and have learned the hard way that it's actually better to just be patient rather than ask for it! My request for patience and contentment is about like that caricature of a little mouse with his head bowed praying, "Please give me patience, Lord – and hurry!"

All too often, I'll get this perfectly reasonable (or even brilliant) idea in my head and want to drop everything and zoom full-speed ahead. Typically when we go on vacation, I get it in my head that we should try to get there as quickly as possible, especially when driving through No Man's Land here out west. When I was younger – especially when the kids were little – I couldn't wait to reach our destination, but lately I've been learning to just enjoy the ride – warts, squabbles, frequent pit-stops, complaints, and all.

So much of our Christian journey is comprised of following and waiting, neither of which comes naturally to us. Our very nature is to push on ahead under our own steam and go wherever we think best. And waiting? Please! Who wants to wait for anything these days – especially us Americans? Yet that's what we're called to do much more often than we care to admit: to wait for God and His perfect timing. Let's face it: waiting is both the easiest thing in the world to do – and also the hardest. Waiting requires us to simply remain where we are and trust Him, to trust that God really is Who He says He is: loving, understanding, and good.

Stand on the corner, I watch my breath freeze in the air
See how it lifts and then vanishes
But I know You're still there
Well, I've got nowhere else to go
'Cause the only life that I know comes from You

How humbling it is to really read the Bible and consider our lives in the light of God and Eternity. How humbling – and downright humiliating – it is to our human notions of self-worth to read that we are mere vapors in this world, flowers or blades of grass that are here today and gone tomorrow.

Sometimes, we can only really acknowledge or process our true fleeting reality when we come to the end of ourselves, like when the rug is yanked out from under us and we fall flat on our backs. Sometimes, we can only see we're really vapors and wisps in the wind when we are being blown about by the wind. Sometimes we can't see how utterly dependent we are until we're broken and helpless.

So many people in this world (myself included) spend so much time running around while giving very little thought as to where they're really going and if they really even want to get there. Getting to that point of "I've got nowhere else to go!" is both liberating and terrifying at the same time. Both when I became saved years ago and more recently with the death of my marriage, my response was about the same: "Okay, Lord – what am I supposed to do now?"

I've come to realize that sometimes that's exactly where God wants us to be: available. Available for His purposes and His Kingdom, not ours. Available to serve and minister to others that He's been watching over. Available for Him to speak to us without being drowned out by all our busyness and running around. Available to be a part of His plan, without having any real plans of our own that would only get in the way and muddy up the waters. Available to be used in the service of the King.

So I stand on the promise,
'Cause I know that the promise is sure
That it comes from beyond us and tells us again
That there's a whole 'nother world
Well, the one I'm in keeps spinning 'round
But I want to stay right here 'cause I found You

Sometimes – and probably much more often than we care to realize – God wants us to just stop moving for once and stay just where we are so He can work in us. Since He's the master chef of our lives, maybe He needs to let us spiritually

marinade for a few days, months, or even years until we're
tender enough (or flavorful enough) to be able to use us. He
marinated Moses in the desert of Midian for forty years and
then the entire nation of Israel for forty years after that.
Why is staying put so difficult for us these days? Why is it
that when we're stuck in traffic that we're often willing to go
miles out of our way through a dozen different side-streets
just so we keep moving? I'll admit it – I'm one of those
people. If I have to be stuck in a car, it should at least be
moving! As it relates to life in general, so often anything is
better than staying put and waiting for something, especially
when it's out of our control!

And yet that's perhaps the only time that God can really
work in us, when we're forced to wait upon Him. He wants
us to come to the end of ourselves and go find Him, and
when we do, what's so bad about just hanging out with Him
and getting to know Him for a while? Isn't getting to know
God better and more intimately what's really of utmost
importance in this wispy life of ours?

Some of the most precious, memorable moments in life
aren't when you're striving to reach a goal or doing
something, but just getting to know someone better. We tend
to remember emotional connections and experiences rather
than achievements, which are usually later replaced by other
achievements. But those deep, personal connections – those
usually last a lifetime. It's about treasuring relationships
much more than accomplishments, and that can be tough in
our goal-driven, go-for-the-gusto culture.

And I can't walk away
  Though the truth is that it can be so hard to wait
When a million voices whisper,
  And they tell me I should leave
Into the shadows that the moon casts
  On these alleys and these streets
But I know that chasing shadows won't get me anywhere

'Cause I've been there

When we rush on ahead of God's plan and take matters into our own hands, we usually foul things up pretty well and foil the good He intended for us because of our own impatience. Some of us – probably many of us – are expert foilers through and through. But when we just wait upon Him, we eventually acquire more patience, trust, and more kept-promises from God. The knowledge that we had very little to do with a particular outcome helps prepare us for future periods of waiting that we can learn from and look back upon, when we can assuredly say, "It was all God, all the time."

Along with the difficulty in waiting, there are so many conflicting voices calling to us every day and pulling us in a thousand different directions. Sometimes we just want them all to shut up for a few minutes so we can get some peace and quiet!

As my marriage entered its final stages, I was bombarded with well-intentioned advice from many different sources, and it seemed like very little of it was all that helpful. So many books and people kept saying "love is a choice" – which it certainly is. However, the way that phrase is used makes it out to mean that love really isn't a choice, that you must love no matter what or you're not much of a Christian. People seem to forget that since love is a choice, the decision to not love is just as valid as the decision to love – it may be the wrong choice, but it's still valid. Also, people seemed to forget that it takes two to get married, but only one to divorce.

But those voices that whispered for me to just give up and move on were some of the worst, and I made a conscious decision to remain where I was and wait for the Lord to continue doing whatever He was doing in both myself and my ex-wife and give Him every opportunity to work in our hearts. Leaving would have been easy, and is often the escape preferred by many people in difficult marriages. But what kind of man abandons his children, his own flesh and blood? What sort of woman tears down her home with her own two hands? What does it say when a person is more attentive and caring to absolute strangers than their own family?

The principles of marriage mentioned in 2 Corinthians 7 call us to maintain the marriage covenant and have peace, regardless of what the other person does (abuse and adultery excepted). But even in cases of adultery, we are to do our best to maintain peace and civility in our homes, and to extend God's love and forgiveness to the perpetrator. Abuse is a far different matter and should not be tolerated for ANY reason. Sooner or later, the couple will either be reconciled and the marriage covenant will be restored, or they won't and the covenant will remain broken. Love is a choice, and sometimes one person chooses to stop loving the other. The marriage covenant is about oneness and intimacy, and if one spouse chooses to leave that covenant, it's pointless to try to force them to stay. That's not a marriage, that's a prison sentence.

So I'm waiting for You Jesus
'Cause I know that those who wait
They will mount with wings like eagles
They will run and not grow faint
They will walk and not grow weary
Their strength will be renewed
Coming from You

If this verse sounds familiar, it's because it's from the well-known verse of Isaiah 40:31 – *"But those who wait on the Lord shall renew their strength; they shall mount up with wings like eagles, they shall run and not be weary, they shall walk and not faint."*

It's so ironic at times that we run ourselves ragged and work to the point of exhaustion (even for God) when all He really wants for us is to wait for Him and be available to Him. We get ourselves all worked up to where we can't even see straight while the whole time He's shaking His head and saying, "Slow down and rest – let Me strengthen you. Stop trying to pull yourself up by your bootstraps and let Me lift you up!"

So I wait
I'm waiting for You
Waiting for You
So come back soon
I'm waiting for You

Waiting is difficult, particularly when times are tough. As the current age of Christendom draws to a close, many are increasingly impatient for the Lord to return and take us home. Many have "Rapturitis" and want to just camp out on a hill somewhere and do nothing while we wait for Jesus to return. Others have the attitude that "It's all gonna burn anyway" and do very little to further the Kingdom. But neither are the attitudes we're supposed to have – in fact, they're both the exact opposite we're supposed to be doing.

Jesus Himself told us in the Parable of the Ten Minas (Luke 19:11-27) that we should keep busy until He returns. There's a ton of work left to do for the Kingdom, and there's simply no excuse for His people to be doing nothing! It doesn't really matter whether you feel called to do something or not – just find something that needs to be done for the Lord and then go do it with all your heart, mind, soul, and strength! And a lot of that time, that "doing something" may be as easy – and as challenging – as simply waiting.

Walks With Rich

22. What Susan Said

"I just wrote a line for Beaker one time. Because, you know how hard it is for guys to tell each other they love each other? We're just, we're so homophobic that we can't even be honest. So I really wanted to tell Beaker I loved him. So I wrote this really stupid song [What Susan Said] for him that I thought was kind of funny. And I included a woman's name, because my audience is so homophobic, that if I wrote a song for a guy they would stop buying my records, and let's face it, I gotta make a living." – Rich Mullins

"What Susan Said" is a song about great friendships, faith, and about what love – genuine love – is really all about. Rich was blessed with a great friend and songwriter nicknamed Beaker, who co-wrote the song. This has been one of my favorites from the first time I heard it, and it's made me think a lot about love and my own friendships over the years.

The main verse of the song is about "how love is found in the things we've given up more than in the things that we have kept," which is completely opposed to our "grab all you can get" culture. I think the reason why love is so tough to hold onto and keep alive over time is because it's all about giving, not merely receiving. We all love to receive because it's easy and wonderful and exciting – but giving takes work and costs you time, money, and effort.

Often time and familiarity pose difficult challenges to love (particularly in marriage) because people tend to get lazy and just stop giving, yet we never stop wanting to receive. Relationships may be many things, but they never really stay in one place, at least not for very long – they're either moving forward or moving backward, increasing or decreasing, growing or dying.

What Susan Said
Proverbs 27:5-10; Philemon 1:12

Two lonely-eyed boys in a pick-up truck
And they're drivin' through the rain and the heat
And their skin's so sweaty they both get stuck
To the old black vinyl seats
And it's Abbott and Costello meet Paul and Silas
It's the two of us together and we're puttin' on the
mileage

And we both feel lost
But I remember what Susan said
How love is found in the things we've given up
More than in the things that we have kept

And ain't it funny what people say
And ain't it funny what people write
And ain't it funny how it hits you so hard
In the middle of the night
And if your home is just another place where you're a
stranger
And far away is just somewhere you've never been
I hope that you'll remember, I was your friend

Two full grown men in a huddle of kids
And they're trying to help them to believe
What is too good to be real
But is more real than the air they breathe

And it's Wally and the Beaver, David and Jonathan
It's the Love of Jesus puttin' on flesh and bone

And we both feel lost
But I remember what Susan said
How love is found in the things we've given up
More than in the things that we have kept
And ain't it funny what people say
And ain't it funny what people write
And ain't it funny how it hits you so hard
In the middle of the night
And I remember what Susan said

And ain't it funny what people say
And ain't it funny what people write
And ain't it funny how it hits you so hard
In the middle of the night

And if your home is just another place where you're a
stranger
And far away is just somewhere you've never been
I hope that you'll remember, I was your friend
I hope you'll have the strength to just remember
I'm still your friend

The song begins with two young men (probably Rich and Beaker) driving a long way in an old pickup truck forming a deep friendship based upon a common sense of humor and their love of Christ. The second verse is about those same two friends years later trying to not only share the Gospel with a group of kids, but living it out in front of them.

The chorus of the song is about both men feeling lost in this great big world and trying to figure out what love is, that love is about giving rather than taking or possessing. The chorus then gets into how after a while away from home, sometimes it begins to feel like just another place where you don't really belong anymore, but you can find love and comfort in your friends.

Next to finding a mate or companion to go through life with, the most precious relationships are between one or two great friends, and those friendships are sometimes very hard to come by. I believe that love and deep friendships are blessings straight from God, and should never, ever be taken for granted. Great friendships are typically based on a common faith or worldview, similar likes and dislikes and humor, and often common paths in life. Friendships grow and take root by sharing, communicating, and investing time and experiences with one another. But great friendships grow by sacrifice, brutal honesty, and a genuine, deep caring for that other person.

Two lonely-eyed boys in a pick-up truck
  And they're drivin' through the rain and the heat
And their skin's so sweaty they both get stuck
  To the old black vinyl seats
And it's Abbott and Costello meet Paul and Silas
  It's the two of us together and we're puttin' on the mileage

Many great friendships begin with one or two things that dredge up strong emotions, such as a shared comical or even miserable experience, and often a shared sense of humor. Whenever I hear the beginning of this song, I remember driving across the South into the Southwest in the middle of summer in 1994 with one of my younger brothers. He had just received a full scholarship to a school out west and we decided to be roommates while I finished up college. The drive was long and sweltering, but it was a great bonding experience for the both of us. The other memorable event at the time was that O.J. Simpson was on the run in his white Bronco through the Los Angeles suburbs and freeways.

One of my best friends was David, my former father-in-law. I'll never forget going over to their house that one summer night and asking him for his step-daughter's hand in marriage. Rather than giving me a straight up yes-or-no answer, he sat me down and read from Ephesians 5 and then explained God's model of marriage. After about fifteen minutes of that (and several tough questions), he granted my request and my sweating abruptly ended. We grew to be very good friends over the years, meeting at Starbucks once or twice a week, watching the news and football, commiserating over American politics and talking about family, church, and work.

David came to Christ late in life (in his mid-fifties) soon after he remarried. And though he was old enough to be my grandfather, we had a great time together and he was still on fire for the Lord when he passed away a few years ago. At nearly the last minute, he decided to go to Israel with me in 2010 and we toured the Holy Land together and had the trip of a lifetime. He used to read the Scriptures every Christmas Eve before the presents were exchanged, and then I took over for him several years ago. Ironically, his wife divorced him about two years before he passed, and then our marriage began ailing soon after she remarried.

His death was the first one that really hit me hard, and I can still feel echoes of him at church, at the Starbucks we used to frequent, and at Standley Lake across from where he lived. We used to walk down to the dock to watch the boats and the two-inch waves, and he could always tell if the lake was higher or lower than it should be. It feels very strange at times, almost as if he's not really dead, but simply away for a long time. I believe that's the way God wants us to view the death of our loved ones, particularly the death of fellow believers – that they're not really gone in the eternal sense as much as they've just gone on ahead of us. Our loved ones in Christ have crossed the Jordan and are now dwelling with the King in the Promised Land, and one day, our number will be called and we'll be shepherded across that River too.

And ain't it funny what people say
And ain't it funny what people write
And ain't it funny how it hits you so hard
In the middle of the night
And if your home is just another place where you're a
stranger
And far away is just somewhere you've never been
I hope that you'll remember, I was your friend

As my marriage really began to crumble, something I was completely unprepared for was the intense emotions that would suddenly strike without warning, and often in the most inconvenient places and times. For a good month or two, I would be sitting at my desk at the office or writing in a library or coffee shop and something would trigger the tears. In the next moment, I would find myself in a restroom or conference room sobbing until the emotions passed. But even though those times have ended, the worst ones are still in the middle of the night when I'm alone with no one but God and my thoughts and my heartache and sorrow.

During that time, the house that was still my home increasingly felt like just another place that I was a stranger in. The same rooms that once rang with joy and laughter soon felt terribly cold, empty, and lonely. Love, family, and friendships create homes and breathe life into them, but when those elements wither and die, home becomes just another strange place – and sometimes a very cold, painful place.

One thing that my ex-wife and I were always blessed with was a good friendship with one another that has survived despite what has happened to our marriage. We have even joked that there's no other person we'd rather go through a divorce with, though there wasn't much laughter about it.

There really wasn't very much anger or bitterness as much as regret and sadness about the reality of our relationship. And though it was very painful and filled with tears for a while, our friendship has remained.

Two full grown men in a huddle of kids
And they're trying to help them to believe
What is too good to be real
But is more real than the air they breathe
And it's Wally and the Beaver, David and Jonathan
It's the Love of Jesus puttin' on flesh and bone

Have you ever wondered why God does things the strange way He does them? If God wants everyone to know that He's real and that He exists, then why doesn't He just show Himself and make it a little easier for us? Why all the cloak-and-secrecy stuff? After all, would it really be that tough to just light up the sky with a huge sign from time to time or shout, "Hey! You down there! I am God and you really should pay attention to what I say! And that whole 'love your neighbor thing', I was serious about that!"

But He doesn't do any of that, does He? He wants people to come to Him because they want to, not because He compels them. He wants people to know that Heaven is real without showing them it's real. He wants people to come to Him by faith, and that means keeping somewhat of a low-profile. He makes Himself known to those who earnestly seek Him: *"And you will seek Me and find Me, when you search for Me with all your heart."* (Jeremiah 29:13)

One of my all-time favorite quotes from Rich is, "I am a Christian, not because someone explained the nuts and bolts of Christianity, but because there were people willing to be nuts and bolts." That perfectly describes what it means for the love of Jesus to put on flesh and bone – people showing others what real love is all about. That's what it means for us

to be the Body of Christ, to let His love and light shine
through us.

And we both feel lost
But I remember what Susan said
How love is found in the things we've given up
More than in the things that we have kept
And ain't it funny what people say
And ain't it funny what people write
And ain't it funny how it hits you so hard
In the middle of the night
And I remember what Susan said

I think it's relatively safe to say that no one really enjoys
feeling lost, or at least not for very long. It's one thing to be
exploring an unfamiliar part of a city and hoping to find
something different and unique, but quite another to be
heading somewhere and suddenly find yourself helplessly
lost.

One of my secret talents that I discovered a few years ago
(the hard way) is my uncanny ability to get easily turned
around and sometimes lost even in places I am relatively
familiar with. It's a gift and also a curse, I suppose, because I
get to see things and places for the first time several times
over! And since my full name is Christopher, when my kids
see that I'm about to head off in the wrong direction or I get
that lost, wandering look of uncertainty, they typically pipe
up with, "Where ya headed, Columbus?" I just smile and
reply, "West!" and then look for the mountains. If it wasn't
for GPS and the Google Turn-by-Turn navigation, who
knows where I would be right now? Maybe that's why I
have an affinity for public transportation at times – don't
bother me with the details, just get me there!

Unfortunately, that's like our attitude with love all too
often – don't bother me with the leg-work and all that
sacrifice, I just want love!

But where can real love be found? Many people seek after it everywhere they go, and they frequently try to find it in the most unlikeliest of places such as bars or nightclubs. But where are most friendships and even love found in life? Typically where you're not looking nor expecting to find it – the same with when you actually do stumble upon it. Love and friendships are these precious gifts that can hit you right out of the blue and fall into your lap, gifts that really can't be manufactured or created – they just happen. That's what makes them gifts. That's what makes them blessings from God.

And if your home is just another place where you're a
stranger
   And far away is just somewhere you've never been
I hope that you'll remember, I was your friend
   I hope you'll have the strength to just remember
I'm still your friend

No matter how far away this life may take you and how much time may have passed, great friends are often able to practically pick up right where they left off years before and barely skip a beat.

I graduated from a small-town high school of about two hundred or so students, about fifty to sixty kids in each graduating class. That's pretty small compared to the schools that have hundreds of students in each class. The great thing about the school was that everybody knew everybody else. That also happens to be one of the worst things about the school too – in small towns, everybody seems to know just about everything about most everybody.

Growing up in and around that small town, I wasn't particularly fond of it at times, particularly since there was this awkwardness between the town-kids and the farm-kids, much the same as with people who live in big cities versus those from Smallville or Mainstreet USA. However, there's

200

usually a pretty good turnout when the class reunions are held, and the last one I attended was my twentieth-year class reunion. Personally, I always thought I'd feel a lot older when I went back for that one, but I'm not complaining. Next year is my twenty-fifth and I still can't figure out where all the time has gone!

Anyway, I hadn't been back to where I grew up since a few years out of high school, and though some of the faces had gotten older, all that old high-school awkwardness was long gone. Some friends were able to pick up right where they had left off after graduation like mere weeks had gone by instead of years. That's a great example of how old friends can often pick up as if they'd only been apart a couple of days rather than twenty to thirty years.

23. What Trouble Are Giants?

"And so, I think courage is the hardest thing to cultivate, you know? The courage to go ahead and do something even though it sounds like it's gonna be stupid. Like the cup thing we do in concert. I mean that's still, people still, everywhere I go, that's, 'Oh, you did the cups! That was so great!' You know? And I go, 'Oh, I'm so tired of that.' And, 'Why doesn't someone else do it?' Because, you know, it's just a lot of people would never do that. Why? I don't know. Maybe because they think it's stupid. I think it's stupid. But I also think people enjoy it. I think all the best things in life are stupid." – *Rich Mullins*

"What Trouble Are Giants?" is a snappy piece from Rich about the classical story of David fighting Goliath and having the right perspective when confronting giants throughout life, regardless of what they are or how big they may seem.

One of the treasures from my last trip to Israel was visiting the Valley of Elah, where the battle between David and Goliath occurred. Also, it happened that our tour-guide was instrumental in excavating the garrison/palace of King David on one of the nearby hills that commemorated the event. Along the western side of the valley is a dried up brook littered with smooth stones, and everyone that picked one up to take home as a souvenir was certain that they were holding the very stone that slew the giant 3,000+ years ago!

(Little do they know that I picked up the real one while they were bragging and squabbling.)

To dig into the story of David and Goliath a little, have you ever wondered why David chose five smooth stones instead of just one? If he knew that God was going to give him the victory, then why did he have four spares? Did he think he might miss and need to reload his sling?

Not at all – the reason David picked up five smooth stones was because Goliath had four other brothers who were probably just as big and strong and terrible as he was (2 Samuel 21:18-22). That day in the Valley of Elah, David was ready to take on not only one giant, but all five! And notice what the story says about how David slew him – he didn't cower or flinch, he ran straight towards him! It's almost as if he knew the victory was already his and he was just running to claim his prize!

What Trouble Are Giants?
Joshua 1:9, 1 Samuel 17:31-51

I'm gonna tell you a story
That you've probably heard
And at the risk of being redundant
I'm gonna tell you something
That may not thrill you
But it could not hurt
Well it comes out of the sacred
Writing of the Israelites
It's the story of David
And how he slew Goliath

Well now the king of his country
He didn't trust in him much
And so to David's alarm
He tried to fit him in his armor

203

But the thing was so heavy
David couldn't stand up
So he left it by the river
Where he gathered five smooth stones
I guess it's safe to say he figured
He wasn't going out alone
He's not alone

What trouble are giants?
What's wrong with being small?
The bigger they come
You know the harder they fall
When you're fighting for Zion
And you're on the Lord's side
Well I think you're gonna find
They ain't no trouble at all (Trouble at all)
No trouble at all
No trouble at all
No trouble

Now there must have been some laughter
Among the Philistines
At the sight of this scrawny little shepherd
Coming out to meet the record-breaking mammoth of a
man
Who was a killing machine
But it didn't shake David
'Cause he was smart enough to know
It's more the size of who you put your faith in
Than the size of your foe

What trouble are giants?
What's wrong with being small?
The bigger they come
You know the harder they fall
When you're fighting for Zion

And you're on the Lord's side
I think you're gonna find
They ain't no trouble at all

For most of my life, I've always been shorter than just
about everyone else, particularly when it came to sports. I
was the boy who was typically picked last in gym class,
except for maybe dodgeball because I was relatively quick
and light-footed. One of my greatest moments of epic
shortness as an adult was when I was chatting with a couple
of other guys in our small group from church a few years
ago. One man was 6'6" and the other was over 7' tall – and
there I was in all my 5'6½" glory, barely able to reach their
armpits!

But does a few inches (or even a few feet!) really matter
to our infinite God? Not at all – though it's often a big deal to
us from our perspective, it's really rather silly and
insignificant if you think about it! Though all the men of
Israel were cowering before Goliath who was twice their
size, if you could have looked down at them from even a
hundred feet above, the difference would be negligible. Now
imagine how insignificant that difference was to God?

What is the true measure of a man or woman? What
makes someone a giant in God's eyes? How much faith that
person has placed in Him – their character, their faithfulness,
their humility, their love and selflessness, their intimacy and
reliance upon Him. Those precious attributes that often
cannot be readily seen with the eyes, but are very clear when
seen with the heart. Men like Job, David, and Noah, and
women like Ruth, Esther, and Mary.

God says in 1 Samuel 16:7, *"Do not look at his*
appearance or at his physical stature, because I have
refused him. For the Lord does not see as man sees; for man
looks at the outward appearance, but the Lord looks at the
heart." Those invisible attributes of character are what

catches God's eye – the quality of one's heart, faith, integrity, purity, and courage – those are what make true giants in God's Kingdom.

Where did David get his great courage, character, and faith from? May I suggest that they were passed down in part from his great-grandmother Ruth? When most people think of the story of Ruth, they usually associate her with her unwavering loyalty to her mother-in-law Naomi when she declared *"Wherever you go, I will go; your people shall be my people, and your God my God."* But Ruth also displayed great faith and character by trusting in God and waiting for Him to provide for her and Naomi, especially in a strange, foreign land. She could have gone back with her own family or chased after another man to replace her deceased husband, but she didn't. She trusted God with her difficult future and cared for Naomi, who really needed her as an older widow. She trusted God even though she faced a life of poverty, loneliness, and being an outcast as a foreigner in Israel.

The story doesn't describe Ruth as a jaw-dropping knockout like Esther, but Ruth had an inner beauty that was just as attractive, if not more-so. Proverbs 31:30 says that *"Charm is deceitful and beauty is passing, but a woman who fears the Lord, she shall be praised."* Though someone may be very attractive on the outside, if their character is ugly, they quickly lose their attractiveness. The reverse holds true as well: people of high integrity and character tend to become more attractive over time, though they may not have changed much physically. The story mentions that Boaz had heard of Ruth and noticed her, but he waited to see what her character was like. He watched her around the other young women and how she maintained her integrity with other men younger and more attractive than himself. Also, Ruth could have sought after any of the other men who were candidates to be her kinsman-redeemer since it was her legal right to do so, but she didn't – it took Naomi's prodding to start that process (and that's proof that mother-in-laws can be a blessing after all!).

In a broad sense, the story of Ruth and Boaz provides an excellent (though admittedly antiquated) model of how dating and courting should be done. What attracted them to one another past the normal outward attributes such as height, beauty, figure, and status? Their mutual faith and character, which is very attractive to people with similar beliefs and integrity. People of faith and virtue should wait patiently upon the Lord and trust Him to bring that special person into their lives, which can often be quite unexpected. They shouldn't chase after marriage as if it's an idol and they certainly shouldn't settle for someone who doesn't believe as they do or someone with questionable character, integrity, or intentions. There should be genuine love, affection, excitement, and passion between them, yet without ever compromising their personal integrity and virtue. People of faith should only marry other people of faith so as to encourage one another in the Lord and build strong marriages, homes, and heritages of faith.

Sometimes acts of great faith and courage can come from the unlikeliest of people. One of my favorite books (and now movies) is "The Lord of the Rings," probably because I've always sort of felt like a hobbit inside. Hobbits are short, stout, shy, and are often overlooked or ignored by the bigger folk. They're picked last for adventures and few outsiders ever take the time to look at who they are inside. Hobbits tend keep to themselves, love growing things, lead quiet lives with their loved ones, have big hearts, and they also enjoy a good pint of beer (or two!). If I were to be a hobbit, I think I would aspire to be Sam Gamgee: faithful, loyal, shy, stout-hearted, innocent, stubborn, and courageous.

The funny thing about hobbits is that everyone always expects them to cower and run away when faced with adversity because of their size, but no one ever, EVER expects them to lead the charge or take on the impossible task. No one ever expects them to step up when others are quarrelling or waffling and say, "I'll do it! I'll do what needs to be done!" At the end of the last movie when the armies of men are surrounded and their doom appears certain, who's running alongside the king charging into the vast armies of Mordor? The hobbits! And who was it that stepped forward at the very beginning of the quest when others were squabbling over who should take the Ring into Mordor? A hobbit! When hobbits (or shorter people in general) reveal their courage against giants and other insurmountable odds, they can inspire just about anyone! Why did J.R.R. Tolkien make hobbits – the most unlikely of heroes in Middle Earth – the protagonists in his stories?

The spiritual truth that Tolkien fictionalized is that God quite often chooses the "least" to be a part of His Family. Though His offer of salvation is available to everyone, God delights in bringing the outcasts, rejects, and the ones nobody else wants, those who are always picked dead-last. Throughout the Old Testament, God always used the most unlikely of heroes to help His people, such as Moses, Gideon, Saul, David, and a whole host of others we would never choose. In the New Testament, Jesus spurred the so-called "righteous" Pharisees in favor of society's outcasts who had ears to hear, eyes to see, and broken hearts yearning to be healed. Jesus called the sick, the blind, the lame, the prostitutes, the tax-collectors, and the poor into His Kingdom rather than the rich, strong, powerful, and righteous. Why is that? Why does God frequently do things that don't really make any sense?

Paul gives us the answer in 1 Corinthians 1:27-29, and it's all related to God's glory and His hatred of pride and self-exultation: "*But God has chosen the foolish things of the world to put to shame the wise, and God has chosen the weak things of the world to put to shame the things which are mighty; and the base things of the world and the things which are despised God has chosen, and the things which are not, to bring to nothing the things that are, that no flesh should glory in His presence."*

An uncomfortable question that should give all of us pause (especially in the healthy, wealthy West) is whether God still prefers those the rest of the world rejects. Does God really delight in the tall, handsome, charismatic speakers (and writers) who can draw thousands to their churches every Sunday or sell millions of books? I don't think so – I think most of them have their reward and will never have His. I can almost picture the Lord sitting on His throne and waiting for the world to finish picking their "winners" so He can scoop up all the leftovers, rejects, and outcasts, to draw them to Himself and delight in them as they delight in Him. In God's creation, He is the Beginning, the End, the Center, and everything in between – not us. Though we are indeed a part of His Story, it's never about us. We are never the center of this universe…God is.

How very different the world would look if our physical height and our outward appearance matched that of our inward character and our hearts? How different would our churches look if all the masks were peeled off and we could see just how broken and desperate – or unbroken and self-sufficient – we really are inside? How much easier it would be to tell what a person was like if their outward appearance was consistent with their inward character and heart-attitudes? But unfortunately it rarely does – but it will someday when we are given our glorified bodies in the Resurrection.

Along with the first shall be last and the last shall be first, maybe the tall will be short and the short shall be tall. For those of us who are vertically-challenged, that would be wonderful!

24. When You Love

"We are blemished people, and in order to love anybody, in any way, we have to expose that part of us that we'd rather keep hidden. Our own selfishness, our own fears, our own hang-ups, and it's embarrassing. So humiliating. But you keep on loving." – Rich Mullins

"When You Love" is one of those bouncy, upbeat songs of Rich's that's practically impossible to stop your feet from tapping to whenever you hear it playing. The song is about loving even when it's not going very well and being thankful even when it's tough. In this life down here on earth, attitude really is everything – or at least close to everything. What differentiates those who hang their heads in defeat from those who hold their heads up high even though they lost the race? Attitude.

My first roommate after leaving home had this framed plaque that I came to cherish and then eventually memorized. At the time I had no idea who the author was, but his words rang deep within me, especially since I had felt like a complete failure after dropping out of that first college and disappointing most of my family:

"Nothing in the world can take the place of persistence. Talent will not; nothing is more common than unsuccessful men with talent. Genius will not; unrewarded genius is almost a proverb. Education will not; the world is full of educated derelicts. Persistence

*and determination alone are omnipotent. The slogan
'Press On!' has solved and always will solve the
problems of the human race." – Calvin Coolidge*

Failure is just as much a part of life as success is (if not
more so), and often our failures lead to our eventual
successes. In fact, the vast majority of people who are
viewed as successful failed repeatedly for years – sometimes
even for decades – before they succeeded. The dirty little
secret is that very few of their failures are ever remembered,
but their successes sure are. But if they would've given up
after yet another failure, they would've never had that
success.

The same is true with love – if we just give up after being
dumped, heartbroken, or even divorced, all we're left with is
another failure and the opportunity or "success" for real love
is eliminated. If we give up on our kids, we extinguish any
hope of them turning around. If we give up on our marriages,
we kill any opportunity for God to work in our hearts. If we
give up, we fail...

We are to never give up – especially with matters of the
heart – never, ever, EVER!

When You Love
Psalm 92:1-3; Psalm 116:16; Dan 4:34; Matt 7:13-14; Matt
11:28-30; 1 Cor 7:21-24; 1 Thess 5:16-18

*There are things you can pray in your prayers
    That you can't sing in your songs
It's like the dreams that lovers share
    When they're safely resting in the promise of a love that
lasts
Though it leads them on to walk a steeper path
    And so sometimes you pray and sometimes you sing
And when you love you thank the Lord for everything*

211

There's a rest you can find in your work
    That you can't get out of sleep
And there's a healing that may hurt
    And there's a war that must be waged for peace
It don't come ready-made
    And if you wanna be free you must become a slave
And so sometimes you work and sometimes you rest
    But when you love you know it all works out for the best

Oh, when you love (When you love)
    Oh, when you love (When you love)
Oh, when you love (When you love)
    Oh, when you love (When you love)
Oh, when you love

There are things you can sing in your songs
    When you've learned them in your prayers
And there's a rest that makes you strong
    For the work that you've been called to share
In with the sons of Light
    And if the Lord should tarry long enough you just might
See that the times were good
    Although the times were hard
And when you love you know you've got to thank the Lord

When you love (you gotta thank the Lord)
    You gotta love the Lord
When you love
    You gotta love the Lord

More often than not, this world is a tough place, and this life we've been given just doesn't run smoothly or easily much of the time. But rather than just accepting our lot in this life and choosing to make the best of it, most people

212

fight to make their lives easy and carefree with every ounce of their being (myself included!). Particularly in the West, we have no patience for much of anything these days, and it shows in our frequent bad attitudes, short tempers, and lack of gratitude – especially given all the common conveniences we're surrounded with that the vast majority of the world would consider to be luxuries.

For whatever reason, sometimes the hardest times can produce the fondest memories. That project at work you never thought you would survive becomes one of the greatest moments in your career. Getting married, giving birth, and raising children are among the hardest, most stressful times in life – but are also the greatest and most rewarding.

This life is full of fascinating dichotomies: to succeed, you must fail first (and repeatedly!); to get real rest, you must work hard; to have lasting peace, sometimes there must be war; and if you want to be free (in Christ), you must become a slave. To become found or saved, you must become lost first; if you want to be loved, you must love first; and if you want to be rich in God's Kingdom, you must become a pauper down here. Will we choose the temporal or the eternal? Will we choose the false wealth that is all around us or the true riches that cannot be bought? Will we choose to focus on our failures of the past or lift up our eyes and trust Him with our future?

Just as the Lord can fling a fistful of dust into the air, give it a little puff, and create a dazzling sunset, that same God is able to bring beauty from even the worst ashes in our lives, though it often remains a complete mystery how He does it. But He is faithful and true, and He has promised to give us a future and hope even in the midst of our brokenness:

"For I know the thoughts that I think toward you, says the Lord, thoughts of peace and not of evil, to give you a future and a hope." (Jeremiah 29:11)

25. Wounds of Love

*"Anyone who's ever been in love's been wounded by it.
My thing is, if you're going to be wounded by something, it
might as well be by love. And if you are too scared of being
wounded to love anybody, then you're worse than wounded.
You're dead. And so, this [song 'Wounds of Love'] is sort of
a blessing you're giving to someone who's far away from
you, someone you want to be with, and you say to them 'Hey,
there's gonna be some hurt in life. It's either gonna be
inflicted on you by someone you love, or it's gonna be
inflicted on you by yourself. I hope it comes to you through
someone you love.' The real tragedy in life would not to be
wounded by love, but it would be to have never loved
because you were so afraid of being wounded. The real
tragedy in life would have been to have missed life because
you were afraid of dying." – Rich Mullins*

"Wounds of Love" is one of Rich's slower songs and
paints a picture of him looking out over a city in the middle
of the night and thinking about someone he deeply cares out,
but they're far apart as the long night settles in. Then he
starts praying and pouring out his feelings and heart to God,
to watch over that other special person and keep them safe
and close to Him. I find myself praying this song a lot lately,
though I don't know her face or even her name yet – but I
know her heart, the heart that beats for the Lord.

This is one of those songs that most people can relate to,
because there's always someone that's far away that you

care about, someone who always needs an extra helping or two of divine protection and love when you can't be there with them.

Wounds of Love
<u>Hebrews 4:16; Hebrews 11:6</u>

It's a quarter 'til tomorrow
  And it's only half past yesterday
The here and the now
  Done come and gone
It's gone away

And the moon over Atlanta winks
  And nods its head for a long good night
And I don't know where you are
  And I don't know how you're sleeping
But I sure do hope that you're alright

And may the angel of His presence keep your heart
  And when your prayers give flight to your dreams
May the only scars you see on their wings
  Be the wounds of love
Be the wounds of love

The bottle is still so full
  There's no one here to turn the tap
So much in me wants to reach out and hold you
  But you're so far away I can't do that

And the dark comes through these windows on the wind
  Makes those votives glow more brilliantly
Well, if passion can lead to prayer
  Maybe prayer can give us faith
And if faith is all we've got

Then maybe faith is all we need

And may the angel of His presence keep your heart
  And when your prayers give flight to your dreams
May the only scars you see on their wings
  Be the wounds of love
Be the wounds of love
  Wounds of love

And the moon over Atlanta winks
  And he nods his head for a long good night
And I don't know where you are
  And I don't know how you're sleeping
But I sure do hope to God that you're alright

And may the angel of His presence keep your heart
  And when your prayers give flight to your dreams
May the only scars you see on their wings
  Be the wounds of love

Because the city is specifically mentioned in the lyrics, this song always brings back memories of living in Atlanta when I started college again after leaving Florida. It was the first big city that I lived in and I remember being awed at how huge everything was and how many people lived there, especially after growing up in a small rural area in the Midwest. I had sold my car right before I moved there and took the subway (and buses) to get around – talk about an instant culture-shock! But many fond memories were created there, and I quickly grew as a result of those experiences.

One emotion that just about everyone has experienced to one degree or another is love. It's universal. And the love that's the most intense, the deepest kind of love is the love that wounds you. If you haven't been wounded by love, then you just might not have experienced real love yet. Real love always costs you something, and don't think for a minute that it won't!

Love is vulnerability, tenderness, soft-heartedness, and sometimes plain old stubbornness and tenacity. Love is the emptying of yourself and giving your heart and affection to someone (or something). When your love is reciprocated, that love is amplified and grows in return. Contrarily, when your love is not reciprocated, it just hurts or can even break your heart. Over time, when love is unrequited or not returned (particularly romantic love) that love can wither and shrivel up, and those wounds can often transform that emotion into something else such as scorn or even hate. That in itself can open deeper wounds, and then often bitterness will set in and can easily grow until it festers to the point where it becomes an all-consuming cancer of the soul.

What – or rather Who – can heal us of our broken hearts and drain away all that bitterness from the wounds of being unloved or rejected? The love of Jesus Christ. Sometimes the love of others can help heal our hearts too, but never as fully, completely, and deeply as His pure, selfless, unfathomable love. Jesus knows every bit of hurt we feel and yearns to take our burdens from us and heal our broken hearts.

Jesus sees the very depths of our souls and knows things about us that even we ourselves aren't aware of. Sometimes we can't articulate or even identify that peculiar ache in our hearts, but He can. As we give our hurts and sorrows over to Him and He frees us of our burdens, often those deeper, older hurts that have been long-buried are dredged up and brought to the surface. The love of Jesus is like the Roto-Rooter of our clogged souls, and He will not stop until our hearts are free and flowing with love – His love. And all we have to do is let Him and yield to His working within our hearts.

And the dark comes through these windows on the wind
Makes those votives glow more brilliantly
Well, if passion can lead to prayer
Maybe prayer can give us faith
And if faith is all we've got
Then maybe faith is all we need

Something I've always had a difficult time with is praying. I think many Christians can relate to that – and I'm not really even speaking of praying publicly. Quite often when I would close my eyes to pray, I would never really know what to say, and it always felt like I was reciting a laundry-list of petitions and requests (as if God really needs me to read it out loud to Him!).

But then came the trials in my personal life, and over the last few years, I have learned to pray. The times I've felt closest to the Lord have been during the darkest times, the nights that felt like they would never end, those days when I would dread even getting out of bed to muck through another day.

Prayer isn't about just reciting a list or petitioning God; prayer is about being open and honest and vulnerable with Him. Prayer is about praising your Maker and Savior and being real with Him. Prayer is about meeting God right where you are – disappointments, wounds, and all. Prayer is about pouring out your very heart and soul to God, confessing your sins and failures and fears to Him and pleading with Him to help you. Prayer is about conforming your heart to His and Him helping you see what He is doing not only in your life, but in those around you – particularly those you're praying over.

Never in a million years did I want to experience the death of my marriage, but through it I learned to pray. I learned to love better and more deeply, and I am a better man because it drew me closer to Christ. My heart has been broken and I am finally soft enough for the Potter to mold and shape me for His purposes rather than my own. Sometimes – many times – that's what it takes to break up the hardened clay of our scorched hearts. While I wish I wouldn't have had to go through that painful experience, perhaps that was the only way He could really get through to me. And for that, I am eternally grateful.

And may the angel of His presence keep your heart
*   And when your prayers give flight to your dreams*
May the only scars you see on their wings
*   Be the wounds of love*

Though the heavens may be shaken and the world collapse all around us, those who are called by His Name must remain faithful and continue to love with all our might. We Christians are to be known not by our politics, opinions, or affiliations, but by our faith, hope, and love – the greatest of these being love (John 13:35, 1 Corinthians 13:1-13):

"Though I speak with the tongues of men and of angels, but have not love, I have become sounding brass or a clanging cymbal. And though I have the gift of prophecy, and understand all mysteries and all knowledge, and though I have all faith, so that I could remove mountains, but have not love, I am nothing. 3 And though I bestow all my goods to feed the poor, and though I give my body to be burned, but have not love, it profits me nothing.

Love suffers long and is kind; love does not envy; love does not parade itself, is not puffed up; does not behave rudely, does not seek its own, is not provoked, thinks no evil; does not rejoice in iniquity, but rejoices in the truth; bears all things, believes all things, hopes all things, endures all things.

Love never fails. But whether there are prophecies, they will fail; whether there are tongues, they will cease;

whether there is knowledge, it will vanish away. For we know in part and we prophesy in part. But when that which is perfect has come, then that which is in part will be done away.

When I was a child, I spoke as a child, I understood as a child, I thought as a child; but when I became a man, I put away childish things. For now we see in a mirror, dimly, but then face to face. Now I know in part, but then I shall know just as I also am known.

And now abide faith, hope, love, these three; but the greatest of these is love."

One of the most challenging times for me to love was when my marriage was ending and we were going through the painful divorce process. At first, I kept making excuses for why I had every right to stop showing love to my wife, but the Golden Rule is not conditional. We are to love those around us regardless of what is happening between us, regardless of how hard it may be, and regardless of how much they have hurt us. Perhaps the greatest lesson I've learned over the last few years is how to love even when it hurts – especially when it hurts very deeply.

Real love always costs you something. Real love is all about sacrifice, and sacrifice is never without pain and suffering. Real love is about putting that other person ahead of yourself for their own good, not yours. Real love wounds – but real love is eternal. Those moments of selfless, genuine love will be the gemstones in the crowns that we will one day lay at His feet.

From the Author

Thank you for reading this book and learning more about some of the lesser-known songs of Rich Mullins, along with what they personally mean to me. I wrote most of the first draft of this book in a library in Salt Lake City after it became clear my marriage was ending. The second draft was finished in Colorado Springs just after the divorce papers were filed. It wasn't a very pleasant time in my life, one of brokenness and searching and the start of healing – but I'm thankful because nevertheless, I know that God will use it for good someday.

As mentioned earlier in the Foreword, this was one of those books I never planned to write, but it was one that simply had to be written. Along with sharing what these songs personally mean to me, writing this book has helped me begin to heal and has given me the opportunity to share my heart with an audience that I have not connected with before, namely other Rich Mullin's fans and ragamuffins.

Rich experienced a tremendous amount of heart-wrenching pain in his life, and it frequently was expressed through his music. By opening himself up and making his hurts and struggles known through his songs, he has been able to help countless others with similar struggles and heartaches. Many of those same "inexpressible sighs and groanings" we all feel have been wonderfully articulated in his music. And though Rich is no longer here on this earth, his music is still touching many hearts and being used by the King.

I sincerely hope this book – a small tribute to Rich Mullins, my fellow ragamuffin and disciple of Jesus Christ – has been a blessing to you. I hope it will encourage you and draw you closer to the Lord, to want to know His heart better and love Him more deeply and fully.

I'd like to close with one of Rich's best quotes about living life to the fullest and keeping a loose hold on this world:

"So go out and live real good and I promise you'll get beat up real bad. But in a little while after you're dead, you'll be rotted away anyway. It's not gonna matter if you have a few scars. It will matter if you didn't live. And when you wash up on that other shore, even though you've been disfigured beyond any recognition, the angels are gonna see you there and they'll go, 'What is that? We're not even sure if it's human.' But Jesus will say, 'No, that's human. I know that one.'" – Rich Mullins

Song and Copyright Information

I'd like to extend a heartfelt thank-you to KidBrothers.net for maintaining the best Rich Mullins website on the Internet. Thank you for all your efforts and years of service in keeping the music, writings, and legacy of Rich Mullins alive and available.

All the Way My Savior Leads Me
Album: The World As Best As I Remember It, Volume II
Song/Lyrics: Fanny J. Crosby and Robert Lowery
Copyright: 1992 - Edward Grant, Inc., Public Domain

Be With You
Album: Pictures in the Sky
Song/Lyrics: Rich Mullins and Justin Peters
Copyright: 1986 - Edward Grant, Inc., 1986 - River Oaks Music Company

Both Feet on the Ground
Album: Rich Mullins
Song/Lyrics: Rich Mullins and Niles Borop
Copyright: 1985 - Edward Grant, Inc.

Boy Like Me / Man Like You
Album: The World As Best As I Remember It, Volume I
Song/Lyrics: Rich Mullins and Beaker
Copyright: 1991 - Edward Grant, Inc. and Kid Brothers of St. Frank Publishing

The Breaks
Album: Brother's Keeper
Song/Lyrics: Rich Mullins

Copyright: 1995 - Edward Grant, Inc. and Kid Brothers of
St. Frank Publishing

Calling Out Your Name
Album: The World As Best As I Remember It, Volume I
Song/Lyrics: Rich Mullins
Copyright: 1991 - Edward Grant, Inc.

Elijah
Album: Rich Mullins
Song/Lyrics: Rich Mullins
Copyright: 1983 - Meadowgreen Music Company

Growing Young
Album: The World As Best As I Remember It, Volume II
Song/Lyrics: Rich Mullins and Beaker
Copyright: 1992 - Edward Grant, Inc., 1992 - Kid Brothers
of St. Frank Publishing

Hard to Get
Album: The Jesus Record
Song/Lyrics: Rich Mullins
Copyright: 1998 - Liturgy Legacy Music / Word Music /
ASCAP

Heaven In His Eyes
Album: The Jesus Record
Song/Lyrics: Rich Mullins
Copyright: 1998 - Liturgy Legacy Music / Word Music /
ASCAP

Hold Me Jesus
Album: A Liturgy, a Legacy, and a Ragamuffin Band
Song/Lyrics: Rich Mullins
Copyright: 1993 - Edward Grant, Inc.

Home
Album: Winds of Heaven, Stuff of Earth
Song/Lyrics: Rich Mullins
Copyright: 1988 - Edward Grant, Inc.

Jacob and Two Women
Album: The World As Best As I Remember It, Volume I
Song/Lyrics: Rich Mullins
Copyright: 1991 - Edward Grant, Inc.

Land of My Sojourn
Album: A Liturgy, a Legacy, and a Ragamuffin Band
Song/Lyrics: Rich Mullins and Beaker
Copyright: 1993 - Edward Grant, Inc., 1993 - Kid Brothers
of St. Frank Publishing

The Love of God
Album: Never Picture Perfect
Song/Lyrics: Rich Mullins
Copyright: 1989 - Edward Grant, Inc.

The Maker of Noses
Album: The World As Best As I Remember It, Volume II
Song/Lyrics: Rich Mullins and Beaker
Copyright: 1992 - Edward Grant, Inc., 1992 - Kid Brothers
of St. Frank Publishing

Nothing is Beyond You
Album: The Jesus Record
Song/Lyrics: Rich Mullins, Mitch McVicker, and Tom
Boothe
Copyright: 1998 - Liturgy Legacy Music, Word Music,
ASCAP, White Plastic Bag Music, SESAC, De Cristos
Music, BMI

The Other Side of the World

Album: Winds of Heaven, Stuff of Earth
Song/Lyrics: Rich Mullins
Copyright: 1988 - Edward Grant, Inc.

Ready for the Storm
Album: Winds of Heaven, Stuff of Earth
Song/Lyrics: Dougie MacLean
Copyright: 1985 - Limetree Publishing, Inc.

Sometimes by Step
Album: The World As Best As I Remember It, Volume II
Song/Lyrics: Rich Mullins and Beaker
Copyright: 1992 - Edward Grant, Inc., 1991 - Kid Brothers
of St. Frank Publishing

Waiting
Album: The World As Best As I Remember It, Volume II
Song/Lyrics: Rich Mullins and Beaker
Copyright: 1992 - Edward Grant, Inc., 1992 - Kid Brothers
of St. Frank Publishing

What Susan Said
Album: The World As Best As I Remember It, Volume II
Song/Lyrics: Rich Mullins
Copyright: 1992 - Edward Grant, Inc.

What Trouble Are Giants?
Album: Pictures in the Sky
Song/Lyrics: Rich Mullins
Copyright: 1986 - Edward Grant, Inc.

When You Love
Album: Pictures in the Sky
Song/Lyrics: Rich Mullins
Copyright: 1985 - Edward Grant, Inc.

Wounds of Love
Album: Brother's Keeper
Song/Lyrics: Rich Mullins and Beaker
Copyright: 1995 - Edward Grant, Inc. and Kid Brothers of
St. Frank Publishing

Miscellaneous Quotes are from Release Magazine:

Release Magazine
PO Box 5047
Brentwood, TN 37024

References and Recommended Reading

The information used in this book was drawn from a variety of sources, such as books, DVDs, papers, and the Internet. One of the best websites for Rich's songs, videos, interviews, and other materials can be found at http://www.kidbrothers.net.

The Bible (New King James Version). Thomas Nelson, 1982.

Homeless Man - The Restless Heart of Rich Mullins (VHS). Myrrh Records.

Manning, Brennan. *The Ragamuffin Gospel: Good News for the Bedraggled, Beat-Up, and Burnt Out*. Multnomah Books. June, 2005.

Manning, Brennan. *Reflections for Ragamuffins: Daily Devotions from the Writings of Brennan Manning*. HarperOne. October, 1998.

Mullins, Rich (Author). Well, Chris (Editor). *Rich Mullins: Home*. Voxcorp Inc. January, 1998.

Ragamuffin (Movie/DVD). Millennium Entertainment, 2014.

Smith, James Bryan. *Rich Mullins: A Devotional Biography: An Arrow Pointing to Heaven*, B&H Publishing Group. August, 2002.

Walks With Rich

About the Author

C.W. Hambleton is the pen-name for Chris Hambleton. Chris resides in Denver, Colorado, where he is employed as a software developer and consultant. He has authored more than a dozen books, as well as developed several websites, software applications, and written software-related articles. His other interests include hiking, running, studying the Bible, reading American history and politics, and literally devouring good fiction books. Recently, he has been learning to enjoy classical music, playing the piano, and learning Hebrew.

To learn more about C.W. Hambleton and his other books, please visit his author website at http://www.cwhambleton.com.

Other Titles by the Author

Speculative Fiction Titles
"Out of the Whirlwind"
"The Exchange"
"The Castors of Giza"
"The Cell"
"Endeavor in Time"

The Time of Jacob's Trouble Trilogy
"The Last Aliyah" (Book 1)
"The Son of Shinar" (Book 2)
"The Siege of Zion" (Book 3)

The Sons of Liberty Trilogy

"The Convention" (Book 1)
"The Green Zone" (Book 2)
"The Declaration" (Book 3)

The Days of Noah Series
"Rise of the Anshar" (Book 1)

The HaZikaron Series
"The Seed of Haman" (Book 1)

Non-Fiction Titles
"Our American Awakening"
"The American Tyrant"
"Ezekiel Watch"
"On the Precipice"

Connect with Me Online:
Website: http://www.cwhambleton.com
Blog: http://fictionsoftware.wordpress.com
Facebook: http://facebook.com/cwhambleton
Goodreads: http://goodreads.com/cwhambleton
Twitter: http://twitter.com/chris_hambleton

Author Biography

Chris Hambleton's first book, "The Time of Jacob's Trouble" was published in 2008 and later revised and expanded in 2011 as "The Time of Jacob's Trouble Trilogy" which chronicles the lives of an Israeli family as they experience the Magog Invasion and then the events of the Great Tribulation.

In "The Last Aliyah" (Book 1 of "The Time of Jacob's Trouble"), the tides of war are once again rising against the nation of Israel. Rocket attacks on Haifa and Sderot are increasing, and Israel cautiously prepares a response to a conflict that many fear will never end. And then a decision is made that will change the face of the Middle East forever.

The story of the Rosenberg family continues in "The Son of Shinar" (Book 2 of "The Time of Jacob's Trouble"), in which after the devastation of Israel's enemies in the Magog Invasion, Israel now has enough weapons and energy supplies for seven years. But now, rumors of a great leader and healer have begun sweeping through Baghdad. Has the Twelfth Imam returned? Could he be the long-awaited Jewish Messiah?

The End Times trilogy of the Rosenberg family concludes in "The Siege of Zion" (Book 3 of "The Time of Jacob's Trouble"). In one day, Supreme Leader David Medine has desecrated the Jewish Temple and Israel has fallen under the authority of the World Union. The Great Tribulation has begun and the future of Israel – along with all humanity – hangs in the balance.

After writing the "The Time of Jacob's Trouble" the next book published was, "Endeavor in Time." In this time-travel science-fiction story, Daniel Marks, the Chief Programmer on a cutting-edge research project, suddenly finds himself back nearly twenty years in the past. With his knowledge of the future before it happens, will he be able to prevent another disaster at NASA before Endeavor, the new shuttle is launched? The sequel to "Endeavor in Time" was published in mid-2012 called "The Exchange" in which Daniel Marks experiences a horrible personal loss and embarks on a hybrid-age journey which will cause him to not only question the entire purpose of his existence, but that very existence itself.

In 2010, "The Cell - Twilight's Last Gleaming" was published, a speculative fiction novel that examines America's future a decade after the financial crash of 2008. As America continues to slog through the Great Recession which has yet to end, the conservatives and the churches have been silenced, and law enforcement seems helpless against the growing gangs and vigilante groups. And though the light of many churches have been extinguished, tiny flames of faith flicker to life and begin to grow.

Late in 2011, Chris's first two non-fiction books were published, "On the Precipice" and "Ezekiel Watch." The book "On the Precipice - Hosea Speaks to America" explores America's current problems in comparison to the book of Hosea in the Bible, in which the nation of Israel had turned away from her Scriptural foundations and was faced with judgment. "Ezekiel Watch - Then They Shall Know" provides a comprehensive examination of Ezekiel 36-39: Israel's restoration to her homeland and the massive attack on Israel by Russia, Iran, and the other Islamic nations of the Middle East.

"The Castors of Giza" is the first of several books that fictionalizes ancient history, with the subject of this story being the building of the Great Pyramid of Egypt. In the Fourth Dynasty of Kemet is growing stronger under its ambitious new leader, Pharaoh Khufu. His father, King Snefuru has established a legacy of extravagant monuments and massive building projects, and his son will not allow himself to become a lesser king. With the science of pyramid construction now perfected, Khufu has determined to build the grandest monument of all time: the Great Pyramid.

In Chris's first politically-oriented book, "The American Tyrant" Barack Obama's background, mentors, and presidency are explored. Who is Barack Obama? Where did he come from, what are his values, and where does he want to take the United States of America? Does his vision of America square with those of America's Founders and past presidents? Where are his czars, policies, and executive orders taking us? Could he really be America's Tyrant?

The latest non-fiction book, "Our American Awakening" is another politically-themed book that explores America's founding, decline into Progressivism, and ways to restore

America. What lies ahead for America in the years ahead? What changes can we make today that will improve America for our children and grandchildren?

"Rise of the Anshar" kicks off a new series of novels that are set in the age before the Flood of Noah, chronicling the events that led to the end of the First Age and then the replenishing of the world after the Flood. "The Days of Noah Series" is expected to span at least five novels, though more may be necessary to complete the series.

"The Seed of Haman" is a spin-off from the story of Haman in the book of Esther set in the 21st Century. A Tehran University professor learns of his family's secret and takes up the mantle to renew their ancient vendetta against the Jewish people. Meanwhile, teams of Israeli operatives are embedded deep inside Iran with orders to thwart the uranium enrichment program by any means necessary.

As the prelude to the novel about the Great Pyramid, the novel "Out of the Whirlwind," is an expanded version of the story of Job that begins at the Tower of Babel and ends with the arrival of Abram in Canaan. Who was the man we know as Job, and how did he become the greatest man in all the earth? What happened to him after his trials, and how was his story preserved?

In "The Convention," the first book of "The Sons of Liberty Trilogy," after six years of a failed presidency, the United States of America teeters on the brink of collapse. When the federal government shuts down over another budget conflict, the Sons of Liberty issue an ultimatum to the Capitol to get their act together – or else. As the conflict between Washington and the rest of the country begins to spiral out of control, a group of state legislators sets out to hold a Convention of States in hopes of pulling the nation back from a civil war.

"The Green Zone" is the second book in "The Sons of Liberty Trilogy." As any hope for legal reforms of the Washington leviathan fade, the Sons of Liberty take matters into their own hands and renew their Ultimatum with vengeance. If the terms of the Ultimatum are not enacted by ballot, then they will be by bullet. With an isolated, out-of-touch president coasting through his seventh year in office, the Sons of Liberty set out to make his last few years in office the worst in history.

Chris's latest book called "The Declaration" wraps up "The Sons of Liberty Trilogy" and provides a glimpse into the future of the United States as it starts to fracture. Rumblings of revolution are heard in Texas while Alaska begins to pull away from the Union. Though their militia movement has been destroyed, the Sons of Liberty rise one last time in the name of liberty and justice for all.